what do you do when you're trying to help someone else, but in the process you're hurting ~~you~~ yourself?

A BEST FRIEND OF MINE TAKES ADVANTAGE OF HOW NICE I AM TO HER. HOW DO I CONFRONT HER?

How do I become more confident?

do you know if your friends are really your fr

What if you really like a boy and he goes out with one of your best friends?

What is LOVE?

my dad doesn't have a relationship with me. How do I fix it?

How do you let an ex-boyfriend know that I still have feelings for Him

My best friend and I have
but ever since she got he

How can you tell the difference between puppy love and real love?

If a friend has dated a boy and they break up does that make him off-limits?

I am shy but want to make friends, how can I meet new people without freaking

How do I get my parents to treat me more like an adult?

I FEEL LIKE MY FRIENDS LEAVE ME OUT OF A LOT OF THINGS. HOW CAN I LET THEM KNOW THIS HURTS MY FEELINGS?

What can I do to gain confidence

I just can't get a guy

I always try and change myself, whether from my clothes, make-up, hair, or body. I feel like I always have to change for other people. Any advice?

How can I be strong for my family when a fellow family member is struggling with an addiction?

What do you do when your friends turn their backs on you?

How can you find someone in High School that you can REALLY trust?

How do you handle bullying?

Have you ever been in a situation where you didn't feel good enough for a guy?

How do I try to be myself & not worry what others think?

I want to go to college but I'm not sure my parents can afford it. What should I do?

Ask Elizabeth

G. P. PUTNAM'S SONS • A division of Penguin Young Readers Group.
Published by The Penguin Group.

Penguin Group (USA) Inc., 375 Hudson Street, New York, NY 10014, U.S.A.

Penguin Group (Canada), 90 Eglinton Avenue East, Suite 700, Toronto, Ontario M4P 2Y3, Canada (a division of Pearson Penguin Canada Inc.).

Penguin Books Ltd, 80 Strand, London WC2R 0RL, England.

Penguin Ireland, 25 St. Stephen's Green, Dublin 2, Ireland (a division of Penguin Books Ltd.).

Penguin Group (Australia), 250 Camberwell Road, Camberwell, Victoria 3124, Australia (a division of Pearson Australia Group Pty Ltd).

Penguin Books India Pvt Ltd, 11 Community Centre, Panchsheel Park, New Delhi–110 017, India.

Penguin Group (NZ), 67 Apollo Drive, Rosedale, North Shore 0632, New Zealand (a division of Pearson New Zealand Ltd).

Penguin Books (South Africa) (Pty) Ltd, 24 Sturdee Avenue, Rosebank, Johannesburg 2196, South Africa.

Penguin Books Ltd, Registered Offices: 80 Strand, London WC2R 0RL, England.

Published simultaneously in Canada.
Printed in the United States of America.

Designed by Paul Kepple and Ralph Geroni @ Headcase Design • www.headcasedesign.com
Greg Lauren • www.GregLauren.com

Library of Congress Cataloging-in-Publication Data is available upon request.

ISBN 978-0-399-25448-2 HC 1 2 3 4 5 6 7 8 9 10
ISBN 978-0-399-25449-9 PB 1 2 3 4 5 6 7 8 9 10

PHOTO/ART CREDITS: Elizabeth Berkley stationery designed by Greg Lauren . Pgs. 12-13: "Snow White Painful" painting by Greg Lauren. Pgs. 28-30: sparkling water background photo by Greg Lauren. Pg. 33: Elizabeth photo by Greg Lauren. Pg. 64: photo by Lara Porzak. Pgs. 81-82: background texture painting by Greg Lauren. Pg. 87: photos courtesy of Elizabeth's parents. Pg. 94: (bottom left) photo by Eric Cahan/painting by Lulu de Kwiatkowski. Pg. 95: Glenn Harvey (trees). Pg. 99: stitched heart by Greg Lauren. Pgs. 108-109: photo by Lara Porzak. Pg. 114: BFF charm by Jennifer Fisher (JenniferFisherJewelry.com). Pg. 115: photo strip photos by Julia Keheller. Pg. 116: Friendship Bracelets by Frieda & Nellie, courtesy of A.sweeT. Boutique. Pgs. 118-119: photo by Elizabeth Berkley. Pgs. 126-128: from *The New York Times*, © 2005 All rights reserved. Used by permission and protected by the Copyright Laws of the United States. Pg. 149: photo courtesy of Elizabeth Berkley. Pg. 159: Photo courtesy of Elizabeth Berkley. Pg. 163: stationery by Sanrio/Hello Kitty. Pg. 188: memory art piece by Greg Lauren. Pg. 189: stationery by Cocodot. P. 196: "Cuba Dancer" photo (upper right) by Eric Cahan. Pg. 213: stationery courtesy of Sharla Crow/SEED. Pg. 222: recital photo courtesy of Elizabeth's parents. Pg. 228: photo of Amalfi by Elizabeth Berkley. Pgs. 235-236: Wish tickets by Gianna Majzler. Pg. 240 (and back cover): photo of Elizabeth Berkley by Josh Lehrer. Stationery on pages 51, 75, and 192 provided by Sugar Paper. Photos used under Creative Commons from Playingwithbrushes: Pg. 94 (tattered blank photo) Pg. 95 (trees) Pg. 160 (tree) Pg. 203 (dress ruffles, goats/mountains). Photos © iStockphoto.com: Pg. 11: swan by Borislav Borisov. Pg. 17: Özgür Donmaz. Pg. 18: dress form by Judith Suarez. Pg. 22: tag by Jill Battaglia. Pgs. 28–29: mannequins by Christoph Achenbach. Pg. 35: Weareadventurers (left) A-Motion Media Productions (middle) Izabela Habur (right). Pg. 37: scale by saiko3p. Pgs. 58-59: girl in field by Joey Boylan. Pg. 63: tag by Catherine dée Auvil. Pg. 66: tablet by Blackred. Pg. 76: tag by Parema. Pg. 78: tag by Hans Laubel. Pg. 81: Tomasz Pietryszek (dandelion left) Alexey Avdeev (dandelion right) Kertlis (sky). Pg. 82: Prill Mediendesign & Fotografie (dandelions) Kertlis (sky). Pg. 87: locket by Keith Webber Jr. Pg. 93: tag by Hans Laubel. Pgs. 114–115: Hal Bergman (amusement park) Jitalia17 (beach chairs) Sema Ozenir (feet). Pg. 135: tag by Matteo Rinaldi. Pgs. 142–143: underwater by Marco Crisari. Pg. 156: tag by Matt Knannlein. Pgs. 160–161: Stocksnapper (back of photo) Tobias Ott (typewriter keys) Subjug (gold frame) spxChrome (cracked glass) Shelly Perry (doily). Pg. 163: diary cover by Shawn Gearhart. Pgs. 166–167: plane photo by Vasiliki Varvaki. Pgs. 168–169: sky by Goldmund Lukic. Pg. 183: doily by Vasiliki Varvaki. Pg. 190: torn book cover by Lisa Thornberg. Pg. 194: spxChrome (tag) Nathan Till (photo album cover). Pgs. 196–197: Kertlis (sky) AVTG (dock) Pawel Gaul (lens flare) spxChrome (gold seal) Leslie Banks (report card). Pg. 201: Andrius Kavaliunas (tag) Elemental Imaging (postcard). Pgs. 202-203: Zxcynosure (sky) Joey Boylan (branches). Pg. 207: tag by Elena Moiseeva. Pg. 229: girl diving by Chuck Collier. Pgs. 235–237: 123foto (ballerina) Winterling (watercolor paint palette) Nicholas Belton (chart of the heavens) Jim DeLillo (starfield). Pg. 240: sky by Kertlis.

Printed on recycled paper

1

THE MIRROR

the fairest of them all

the fairest of them all

the fairest of them all

the fairest of them all

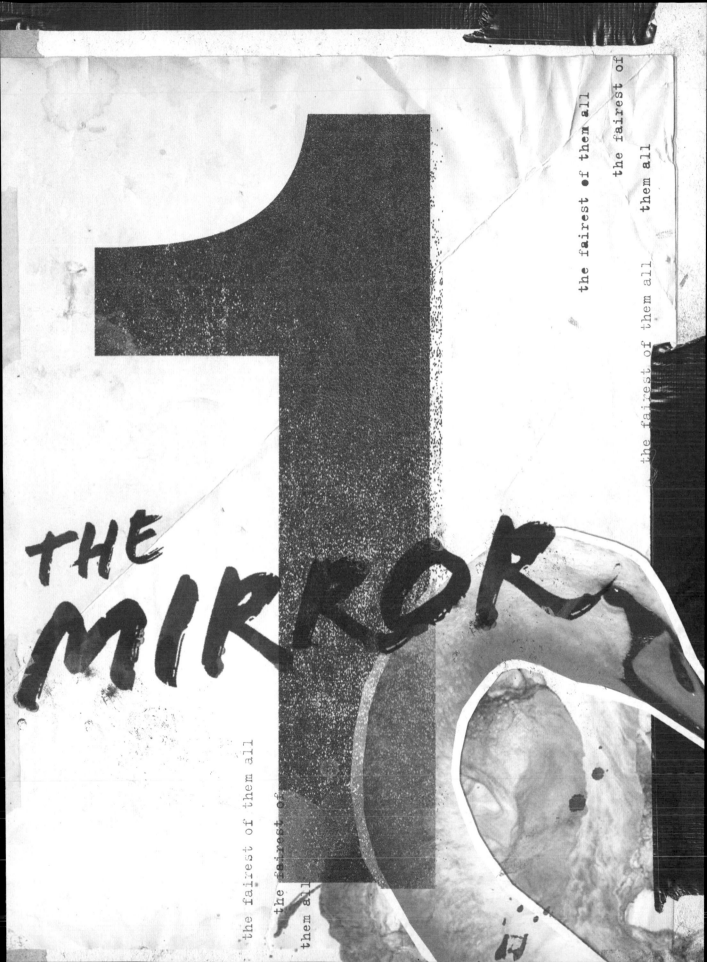

LEARNING TO LOVE YOUR PERFECTLY IMPERFECT REFLECTION

* *

You might be asking, Why begin with the superficial? Why jump right in and talk about looks? Aren't there more important things to deal with? As if our self-image isn't "important"--ha!

The reality is that not loving how we look is one of the biggest issues that can bring us down. In almost every workshop, at least one question comes up about how to deal with feeling unattractive or "less than" other girls in some way. Believe me, I have my own issues I deal with in this area. You might think you're alone in your body or beauty struggles, but trust me: I've talked with thousands of girls across the country, from all different backgrounds, and I can tell you for sure that nearly all of us struggle with these issues in one way or another--even the girls we least expect.

That's why I want to get right to the heart of this whole negative self-image thing here at the very beginning, and bring those secret worries out in the open so that we can all finally break free of them. So let's jump right in and get the two biggest questions you guys have been asking about this out of the way, so they don't have the power to weigh you down anymore. And then we can get to the deeper, juicier stuff that's going on in your minds, your hearts, and your lives.

You ready? I'm with you every step of the way, and so are your new <u>Ask Elizabeth</u> sisters. Here we go...

What do you do when you look in the mirror and **hate** what you see?

"Mirror, mirror on the wall..."

Remember that line from *Snow White*? Wouldn't it be nice if our mirror responded to our reflection with wonderful, kind, loving words of encouragement? *"You're the most beautiful creature on the planet. . . . Wow, those are some gorgeous thighs. . . . Love that amazing stomach of yours. . . ."* We'd all have the best self-esteem on the planet!

Okay, but here we are back in the world of reality, where you've all been admitting that you're not quite feeling that kind of love when you see your reflections. What do *you* say to yourself when you look in the mirror? If you're one of the rare few who automatically respond with only positive thoughts, wow—that's inspiring. Can we please trade brains with you? Because most of us immediately zero in on whatever bugs us the most and nail ourselves. Don't believe me? Take a look. . . .

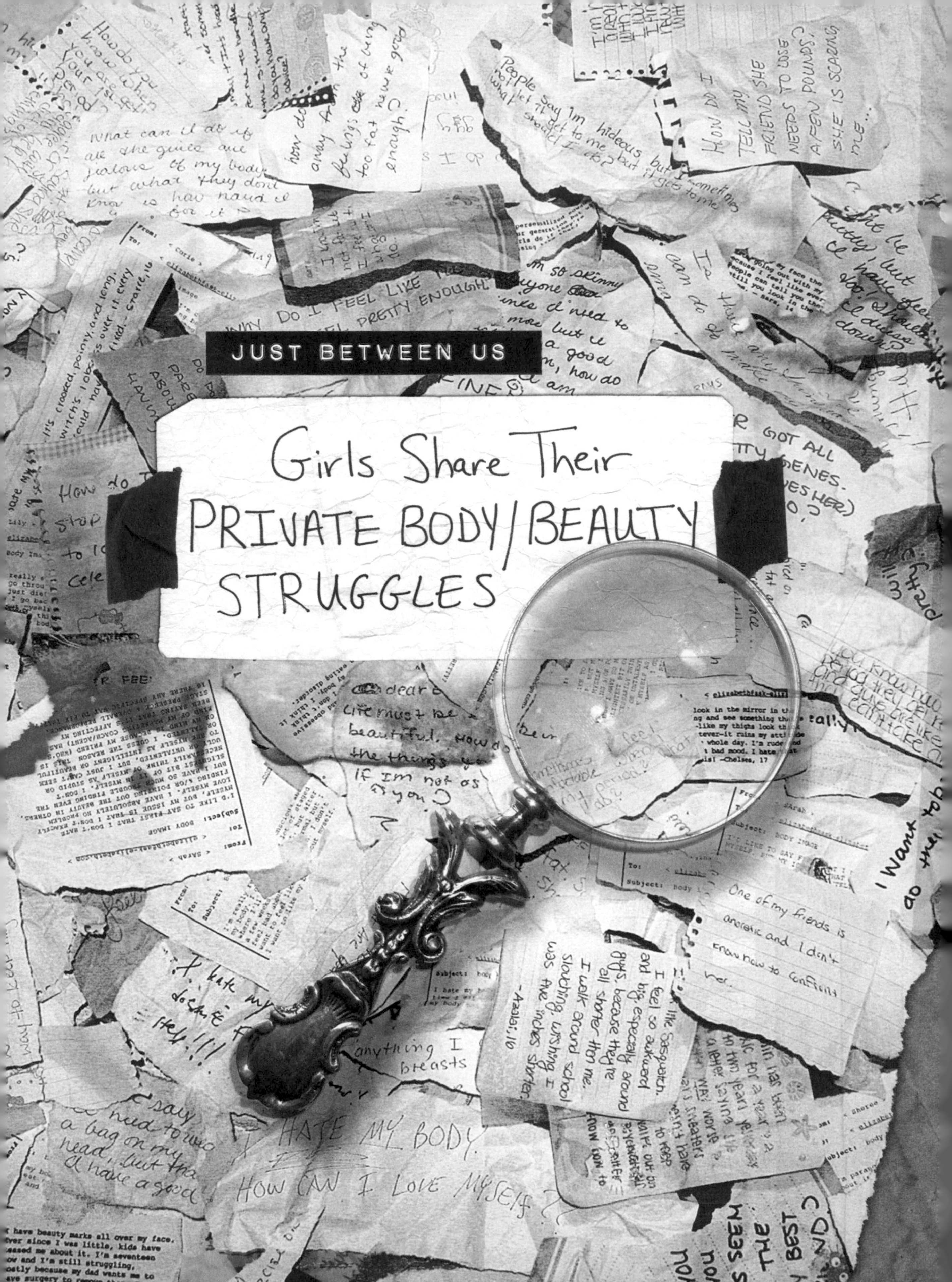

JUST BETWEEN US
Girls Share Their
PRIVATE BODY/BEAUTY
STRUGGLES
How do I TELL my FRIEND SHE NEEDS TO LOSE A FEW POUNDS? SHE IS SCARING ME...
One of my friends is anorexic and I don't know how to confront her.
I HATE MY BODY. HOW CAN I LOVE MYSELF?
I want to do the...

MAN, EVERYONE HAS CELLULITE, RIGHT? I FEEL LIKE THAT SUBJECT IS SO GHASTLY AND TABOO to ADMIT, BUT I HAVE IT... ON MY LEGS.... AND ON MY BUTT... YUP, NO APOLOGIES. I LOOK AT MYSELF AND I WISH I WAS SMOOTH, SILKY, FIRM, AND SOFT, BUT I HAVE SKIN GOSH DARNIT, NOT PLASTIC!

– VANESSA, 17

It's so weird but I wish I had bigger nipples.

– Ricki, 18

To: < elizabeth@ask-elizabeth.com

I had a complete breakdown about my face the other day. It often stops me from going out with my friends or on outings because I feel like everyone is staring at my face. People can tell you they don't see the zits, but still you look in the mirror and that's all you see. – Sara, 14

To: < elizabeth@ask-

I feel like I have hair everywhere on my body.... I'm so insecure about it, it's even on my stomach. I won't wear a shirt that might ride up, even though I have a pretty flat stomach, because I think someone's going to look at me and be like, 'Eww, are you an ape or something?' – Gia, 15

Honestly, I cry whenever I look down at my stomach and see it hanging over the top of my jeans.

-Carina, 15

I hate my nose. It's crooked, pointy, and long, and looks like a witch's. I obsess over it every day and wish I could have it fixed. – Starre, 16

To: < elizabeth@ask-elizabeth.c

If I look in the mirror in the morning and see something that's wrong—like my thighs look thick or whatever—it ruins my attitude for the whole day. I'm rude and I'm in a bad mood. I hate that I do this! —Chelsea, 17

I look like Sasquatch. I feel so awkward and big, especially around guys, because they're all shorter than me. I walk around school slouching, wishing I was five inches shorter.

—Azalai, 16

To: < elizabeth@ask-elizabeth.com

I have beauty marks all over my face. Ever since I was little, kids have teased me about it. I'm seventeen now and I'm still struggling, mostly because my dad wants me to have surgery to remove them. I guess he thinks I would be prettier if I removed them. And that really hurts. —Marta, 17

I hate how big I am. I get really tired of being the fat girl with the pretty face . . . the girl all the guys are friends with but no one dates.

— Ariel, 16

To: < elizabeth@ask-elizabeth.com >

I've had an insecurity with my hips/stomach ever since I was eleven. I would get teased all the time by my older cousins about having 'jellyrolls.' I remember them chasing me, lifting my shirt and saying, 'Let me see yo' jellyrolls!' and pinching my fat. At the time it was a big joke and I'd laugh along, but it secretly upset me. To this day I'm constantly reminded of being the chubby little cousin with the fat rolls. The thought of me being a heavy person still affects me.... I honestly believe that being ridiculed as a kid so much made me obsess over working out today. —Marissa, 18

Any of these sound familiar? Wow, are we tough on ourselves!

Those nasty voices in our heads aren't just our own creation, though; we've got plenty of pressures coming at us to stir them up. We're so used to seeing all these digitally perfected images staring back at us from magazines and billboards that we start to think that's what's "normal." I'm sorry, but how can we not feel insecure next to that? And don't think that every commercial or ad you see isn't somehow creeping into your beliefs and making you feel like you're not enough without their product.

On top of the pressure we put on ourselves, you've all been telling me that the guys in your lives seem to expect you to look like those images, too—yeah, great, like we needed another reason to get down on ourselves!

Some of us have been teased or rejected for being too tall, too fat, too thin, too anything. . . . It's crazy how even one mean comment from someone can stick with us and become what we believe about ourselves. Those voices in our heads saying we're "not enough" don't fade easily, do they?

As an actress, I know the "magic" it takes to make the images look that way, but they can still trigger self-doubt.

When I was younger I used to dream of having beautiful movie-star curves. I was teased for being a tall, skinny beanpole, so thank God one summer the boobs and curves finally arrived...hallelujah! Years later, I had a boyfriend who flat-out told me that he preferred girls without curves. He would actually point out to me girls who had the more boyish body type he liked and tell me how sexy he thought they were. Great for my self-esteem, right?

Suddenly, having curves equaled rejection to me, and so every time I looked in the mirror, I hated what I saw.

I desperately wanted to fit his image of what he thought was beautiful, so I would try to flatten my boobs by wearing sports bras under my clothes, and I started eating less, hoping they would get smaller. I'd stand in front of the mirror, squeezing the skin on my hips, trying to will away my feminine curves. I wanted to feel confident, but all I could hear was his voice in my head telling me that I wasn't pretty the way I was. --XOE

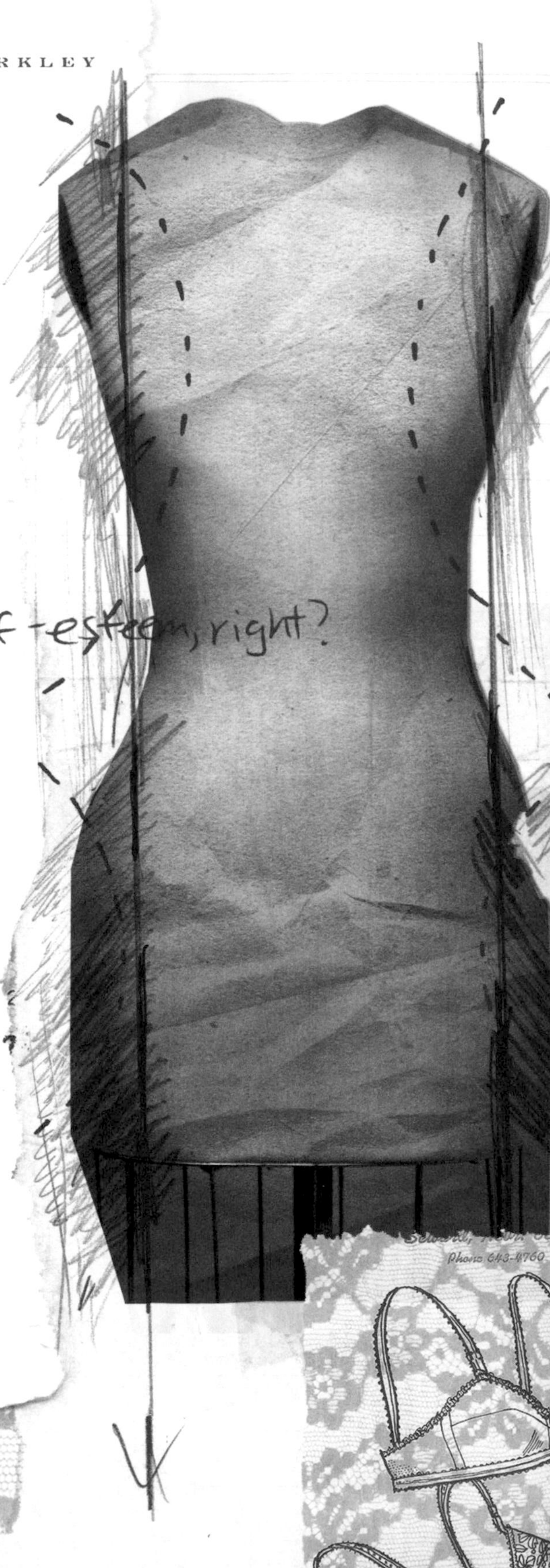

So how did I start to quiet the nasty voices in my head? How do we fight back against these hurtful judgments, whether from someone else or from our own imaginations? I'm here to tell you there is a way.

ACTION STEPS: Ditch the Mirror Drama

"Mirror drama" isn't just about how we feel when we look in the mirror. . . . It's how we feel in our skin every minute of every day. We might not be able to silence those nasty inner voices permanently, but the action steps here will definitely help you turn down their volume each time they threaten to ruin your day . . . your week . . . your life. . . .

♥ you don't have to do any of the action steps throughout the book in order. Just use whatever tools feel right to you whenever you need them.

ACTION STEP #1

Catch Yourself

You know how we just talked about all those different places where the nasty voices can come from (a critical boyfriend, other people in our lives who made us feel inferior, media images, etc.)? Well, it's time to stop letting those sources have power over us, once and for all! There's a way to actually stop these voices in their tracks as soon as they start messing with you, and it's easier than you might think. It's called *awareness.*

Here's how it works: let's say that same old voice kicks in—the one that screams "I'm ugly" or "I'm fat" or whatever else your inner critic loves to say to shred your self-esteem. When that happens, most of us immediately buy into what it's saying and without even realizing it, let that negativity take us down. But right there, in that moment, we have a choice. We can pause, look within,

Bra—Size 30
C & D Cup
Fabric needed:
See Pattern

ew 2
dded)

and ask ourselves: Whose voice is this? Is it mine? Do I really believe this? To become aware of the voice rather than just letting it immediately become what you believe about yourself is so empowering, because it puts the control back into your hands.

Even though this might sound extreme, letting other people's critical voices take over is like brainwashing, and we need to rewire how you think. This step of catching the inner critic is about separating yourself from other people's negativity and getting back to what *you* think. When I was working on getting rid of my ex-boyfriend's critical voice that was ringing in my head, as soon as I'd hear myself think "I hate my curves," instead of going on autopilot and hating what I saw, I would catch it and remind myself that those were his words, not mine. Each time, I would consciously stop myself, "*There I go again . . .* "

Remember, I loved those curves when they first showed up

Ditching the mirror drama isn't about waiting for someone or something else to make you feel better about yourself; you are the only one who has the power to stop it. There is no beauty or satisfaction in looking for your self-worth in everyone else's opinions. The real beauty comes from looking at yourself through your own eyes. Then, from deep within your soul, you will start to see the true beauty in the mirror.

I know that some of you might be saying, "Yeah, okay—but it's actually *me* who thinks I'm too fat, or too short, or whatever." Don't worry, we have ways to deal with that voice, too. Read on . . .

ACTION STEP # 2

"Flip It"

Something you repeat to yourself that activates a new belief.

Flip it: two words that can become your favorite new mantra!

Whenever I catch myself having one of those mean thoughts that I believe is really true, I remind myself I can "flip it," meaning I can choose to change how I'm feeling about myself in that moment. No joke, it's within your power to turn this around. We can re-program our minds, just like we started to do in action step #1, so that when we look in the mirror, we actually start to love what we see instead of automatically tearing ourselves down. You're probably wondering how to do this, right? Hang in there with me, I'll explain.

Negative thoughts have a lot of power. Think back to a recent bad day you had. How many times that day would you say you told yourself something mean? I'm guessing a lot. If you keep telling yourself you look like crap, then that becomes your belief, and whether you realize it or not, your brain is then programmed to seek out other "flaws." It becomes a habit.

The way we break this habit is by creating a command that will stop the flow of those negative thoughts. It can be anything like, "*Stop it*" or "*Do not do this*," "*Knock it off*" or "*No way—this is not happening any more!*" If you had an awful houseguest, would you allow them to keep yelling nasty comments at you? I don't think so! Just like you would need to take care of yourself by showing them the front door, you need to do the same within yourself. So when a mean thought comes up, you can "flip it" by commanding it to stop in its tracks. Behaviorists say that if you want to break a habit, it takes 28 days . . . so let's consider today day one of your new programming. 27 more to go! — ha!

Or you can create your own that works for you.

Telling the negative thoughts to go away isn't enough, though; you also need to replace them with some positive ones. Just like the negative thoughts are contagious, the good news is so are the positive ones. So I want you to try something, okay? The next time you stand in front of a mirror, instead of automatically zeroing in on what you hate, ask yourself, *What do I like about what I see?* C'mon, don't tell me you can't find one thing you like. Appreciating even one feature can start your mental list of positive thoughts flowing, which you can then use to replace the negative ones. By reprogramming ourselves to seek out the positive, we create a *much* better habit.

This might feel a little weird at first, but I swear, it works. This is the secret to rewiring your inner beliefs and building confidence. Don't worry if some days you fall back into your old patterns. You can start fresh any day, any time—it's an ongoing practice.

See why "flip it" can become your favorite new mantra?

PLAY IT UP!

Wouldn't you say you spend more time making sure the body part you hate is covered or hidden than playing up the parts you love? Once you start to appreciate and fully own those features that you like, you can actually put more focus into highlighting them. Let's say you like the color of your eyes; find a shirt or piece of jewelry that makes them pop. If you love your arms, accentuate them--don't be afraid to sport that tank top. See what I mean? You can experiment with different things so you can emphasize what makes you feel like you shine and sparkle even more. XOE

ACTION STEP #3

Take Control of What's Within Your Power to Change

If there's something you can change about how you look that will give you more confidence, I say go for it—no apologies! You don't ever have to feel bad for wanting to look good.

I know we're told all the time by parents and other people who love us that we shouldn't focus on "superficial" things like appearance—that inner beauty is all that matters. And yes, of course what's in our brains and soul matters most, because that's our true essence . . . our thoughts, beliefs, feelings and dreams. But it doesn't have to be either/or. If there's something you can do with your

appearance that can help with self-esteem, what's wrong with that? Nurturing yourself by eating foods that make your body healthy . . . honoring yourself by taking care of your skin and hair or by working out . . . finding clothes that you feel good in . . . it's time to commit to loving yourself enough to make those changes instead of staying in "I hate how I look" mode. Not for anyone else, but for *you.*

So much of our attention is wasted looking to other people to give us those feelings of confidence, but like I said, we have the power and the right to start giving that to ourselves instead. If there are things that are bringing you down to a degree that you are not allowing yourself to socialize or have other joyful experiences, then by all means, start taking steps to change that and make yourself feel better. This kind of self-care and pride is a beautiful gift you can give yourself. This is far from superficial—how you feel about yourself physically can affect so many aspects of how we show up in life.

There are tons of (non-surgical) beauty and body fixes that can help us change the little things that can turn into big things in our minds. Don't worry, you don't have to figure out how to do it all yourself. I've gathered some of my favorite experts from Hollywood and New York City to share their amazing advice. I want you guys to have the best!

Do you feel self-conscious because your skin breaks out a lot? According to Dr. Amy Wechsler, one of the country's most acclaimed dermatologists (and get this—she's also an adolescent psychiatrist), this is treatable. She says, "I know acne can have a big effect on your self-esteem, and those negative feelings can spill over into everything else in your life. But I promise, it isn't hopeless—you're not stuck with it. There are a lot of great ways to get control of it, instead of letting it control your life." On my website, www.ask-elizabeth.com, Dr. Wechsler will give you a tutorial on what causes breakouts and what you can do to prevent and treat them, which can start you on your way to feeling better about your skin.

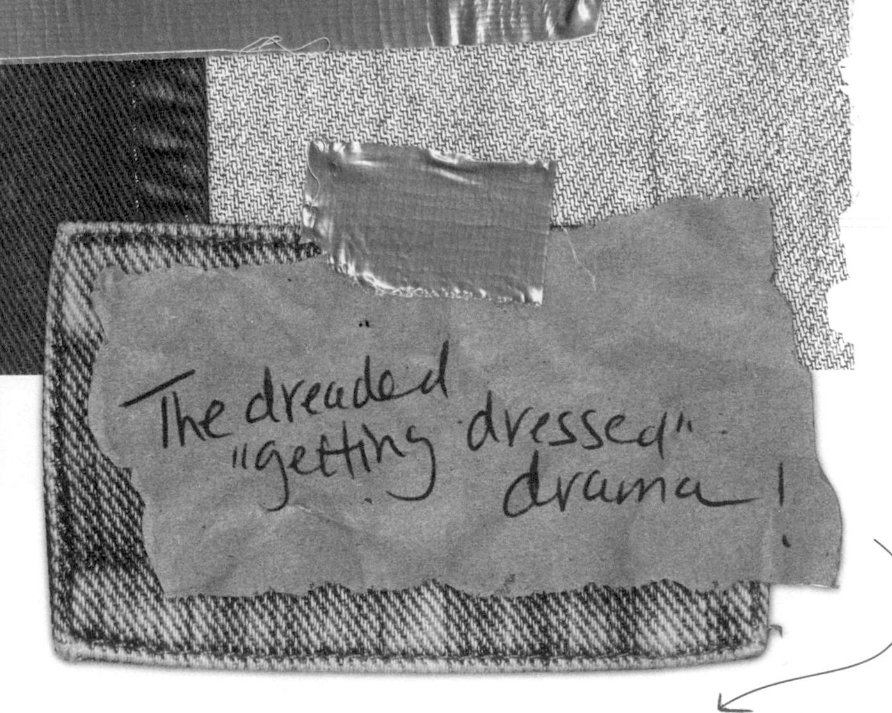
The dreaded
"getting dressed"
drama!

Hate how your clothes look on you? Spend some time in stores trying on different styles and cuts to find what you like; what's trendy at the moment just might not be right for your body type. (Just ask jeans maven Paige Adams Geller, founder of Paige Premium Denim. . . . She'll guide you on my website to find the perfect pair for your individual body.)

Seventeen-year-old Danielle shared how that tip changed things for her: "Every time I tried to wear skinny jeans, I spent the entire day miserable. Even if I was doing something fun with my friends, all I'd secretly think about is how totally uncomfortable I was with them digging into my stomach." Danielle adds, "Finally I just said, 'This is stupid, why am I torturing myself?' So I've stopped trying to shove myself into clothes that don't complement my body type, and ever since I've been so much happier."

I think we can all admit that not liking how we look or feel in our bodies can ruin some of life's most joyful moments.

Since body drama seems to be one of the biggest things I hear you guys say brings you down, I wanted to just give you a little peek here into the amazing advice from celebrity fitness trainer Valerie Waters.

and my girl!!

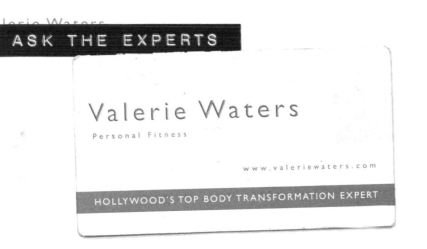

Valerie Waters

Personal Fitness

www.valeriewaters.com

HOLLYWOOD'S TOP BODY TRANSFORMATION EXPERT

on Committing to Yourself

What I always say is that it starts with the desire to want to get into shape. When it goes from "I should" to "I will" in your mind, that's when things start to change. So when you stop wishing and think, *I must do it*, you get a little traction.

And then you want to follow it up with immediate action. Make the first step the easiest one you can possibly take—if you like working out with other people you can take up a sport at school or take a spinning class at a gym, or if you prefer working out privately, get a workout DVD you can do at home, download a fitness program from the Internet; or even just a fitness magazine . . . anything that puts you in the right direction. Then follow it up with another action, to keep the momentum going, like maybe making one tiny change in your diet, like choosing a turkey sandwich instead of a burger and fries for lunch or you can decide to walk to your friend's house instead of having a parent drive you. Fitness is meal by meal, workout by workout, choice by choice. The people who are fit are that way not because they are genetically blessed, but because they make

11693 San Vicente Blvd • Suite 134 • Los Angeles • CA • 90049 • www.valeriewaters.com

Valerie Waters
Personal Fitness

decisions every day to be fit. Think: step . . . step . . . step; if you string enough of those things together, you start to see yourself as someone who lives fit.

The rewards for getting in shape are so much greater than just a better body. I know people wish they could wave a magic wand and be in shape, but you wouldn't get the benefit of what you go through to get there. Getting yourself fit changes who you are. You see that you can follow through, you can make things happen. You get stronger and faster, you will have better balance and mental acuity. All these things make life more available to you. If someone comes along and says, "Hey, want to go hiking?" (or play volleyball, or whatever else), you won't have much fun if you're not in good condition. But if you're conditioned, you have the strength and confidence to try. It's about getting more out of life. I know we want to look good (and there's nothing wrong with that), but we also want to be able to enjoy life and participate in whatever good things come up.

The biggest piece is to *decide*, and then start. And then just keep going!

Trust me, girls. There are days I have to drag myself to the treadmill, but it's the commitment I made to myself that keeps me going!

11693 San Vicente Blvd • Suite 134 • Los Angeles • CA • 90049 • www.valeriewaters.com

Or just ways to empower yourself with healthy new tools to give you extra focus and energy.

You'll find more tips from these experts and many others on the website, including the real deal on how to lose weight the healthy way from Carrie Wiatt, celebrity nutritionist and author of *The Diet for Teenagers Only*, and more.

By taking control of what's within your power to change, you'll look and feel better. Even more, you'll get the added good feeling of knowing you're doing something positive for yourself, and honestly, that's the best confidence-builder there is.

ACTION STEP #4

Learn to Love What You Can't Change

Let's be honest. . . . There is a level of self-acceptance that we do have to get to in order to feel happy, right? If I had a magic quick-fix answer on how to do this, trust me, I'd give it to you. But you don't just wake up one day and—*BAM!*—your self-esteem is rock-solid. It's a lifelong process. How we feel about ourselves can go up and down. There might be skinny days and bloated days, days when you look sparkly and days when you look tired, mornings when you feel confident and others when you feel just plain gross.

I still find new things about myself to criticize... Grrr!

Your new *Ask Elizabeth* sisters have a bunch of strategies and thoughts to help make the path to self-acceptance a little smoother. . . .

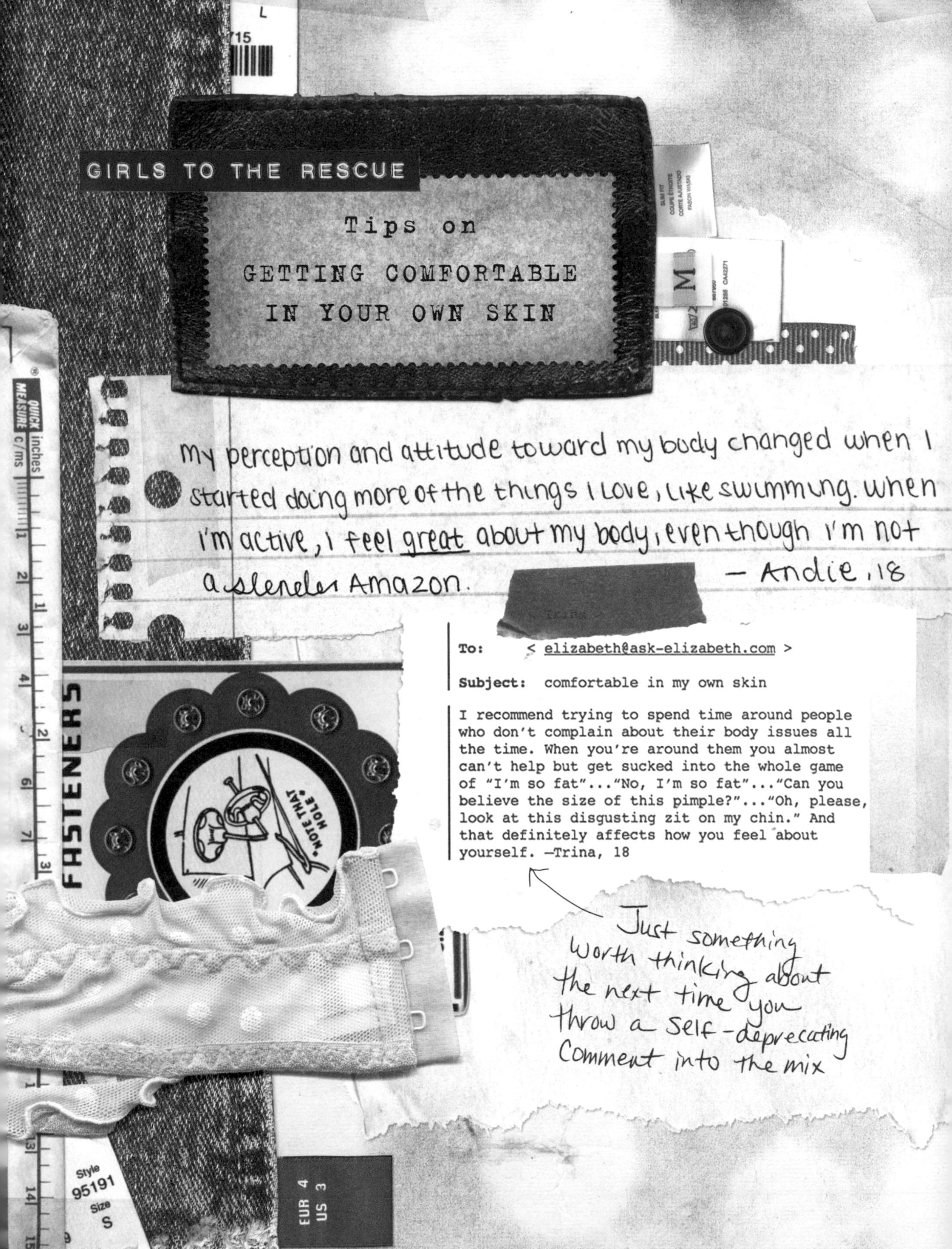
GIRLS TO THE RESCUE
Tips on
GETTING COMFORTABLE
IN YOUR OWN SKIN
My perception and attitude toward my body changed when I started doing more of the things I love, like swimming. When I'm active, I feel great about my body, even though I'm not a slender Amazon. —Andie, 18
To: < elizabeth@ask-elizabeth.com >
Subject: comfortable in my own skin
I recommend trying to spend time around people who don't complain about their body issues all the time. When you're around them you almost can't help but get sucked into the whole game of "I'm so fat"..."No, I'm so fat"..."Can you believe the size of this pimple?"..."Oh, please, look at this disgusting zit on my chin." And that definitely affects how you feel about yourself. —Trina, 18
Just something worth thinking about the next time you throw a self-deprecating comment into the mix

I love it... Fake it till you make it... from the outside inward!

To: < elizabeth@ask-elizabeth

My friend and I were talking the other day about how people's walks say something about them. I'm really insecure, and I feel like I used to walk that way. But I started watching girls who I thought were really confident, how they moved, and I started to emulate it, and I actually started to feel more confident. —Jovana, 16

To: < elizabeth@ask-elizabeth.com >

Subject: Being Comfortable in My Own Skin

I'm overweight, and even if I lose all this weight, I'm still going to be big-boned. I just came to this realization one day: 'This is me... I have to deal with that.' The way I'm choosing to deal with it is to work to lose the weight so I can get to the best version of myself.... That's at least something I can control. —Morgan, 16

I'm kind of flat—like really flat. There's this jerk in my class who wouldn't let me go, and he commented on it all the time. It sounds weird, but making jokes about it myself made me feel better about it. Talking about it out loud with my friends also helped, so it wasn't this big secret I was keeping in. —Liza, 16

Up until ninth grade, I was totally flat. Guys used to tease, "You're a sunken chest: pirate's dream..." but I'd be like, "Ha, ha," but inside I was dying...

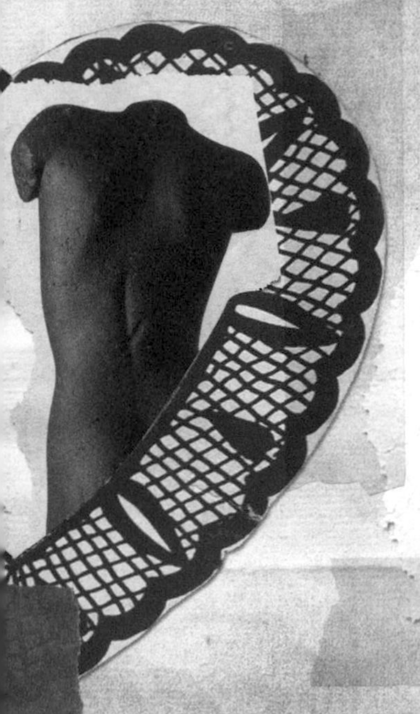

From: < Rica >

To: < elizabeth@ask-elizabeth.com >

Subject: Comfortable in your own skin

I think you just have to be kind to yourself. Definitely the most vicious criticisms I have are, interestingly enough, reserved for me. I would never dare think for a minute to call a girl 'ugly' or 'fat,' but when it comes to myself, I don't hesitate. At a point I started to wonder, how can we be so nice to other people and then treat ourselves like crap?
—Rica, 15

Be your own best friend!

Its corny... but I actually like to write notes of encouragement to myself. Whenever I'm bummed out about how I look or I think I'll have a bad day, I write a note and tape it to my bedroom wall. I've been known to write "You look amazing" or "You'll kick ass today!" Itś really silly, but it keeps me sane. —Haley, 15.

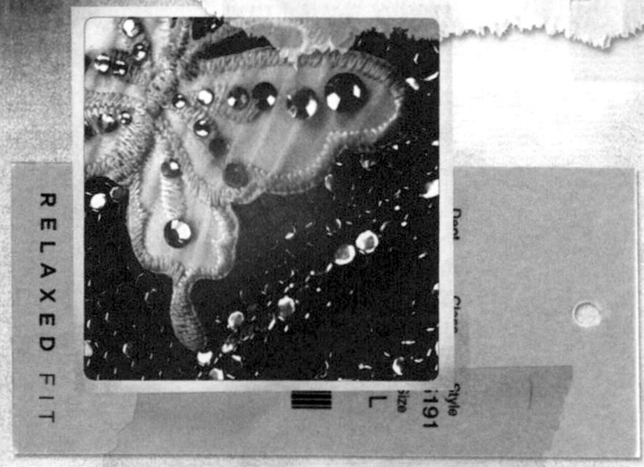

ACTION STEP # 5

Embrace Your Imperfections

We need to give ourselves a break here and get off our own backs. It's okay not to be perfect! Every single one of us has imperfections. I know that the big fear is that other people will see or judge our "flaws"—it can feel like there's a gigantic microscope on us at all times—but it's funny how small and insignificant these things actually seem to everyone else.

I want to share a story with you from my amazing BFF Seane Corn. Seane and I met twelve years ago when I was a student in her hugely popular yoga class, and since then we've helped each other through so many of life's highs and lows. I am so grateful for her brilliance, and I wanted to pass along her wisdom to you so you can be as lucky as I am to have her to learn from. She has a special story about how she learned to live with those physical "flaws" we feel stuck with.

Here you go . . .

"What do you do when you look in the mirror and hate what you see?"

SEANE CORN

My BFF Talks About Living with Our Imperfections

When I was six months old, I crawled into something very sharp, cutting a gash through my right eyebrow and leaving me with a small but very noticeable scar. When I was twelve or thirteen I became very self-conscious about how it seemed like I had three eyebrows instead of two. It made me feel different and imperfect at an age when all I wanted was to look like everyone else.

At fourteen I discovered Maybelline eyebrow pencil and began covering my scar every morning before I went to school. That became my morning ritual every day until I was eighteen and moved to New York City. One morning my roommate saw my face makeup-free and said she thought my scar was so cool and beautiful, and encouraged me not to cover it. That night I went out with it exposed for the first time in years, and all my friends remarked on it in such a positive way. They thought it was so unique.

I remember looking at my face differently from that point on, realizing that this slight imperfection gave my face character. It didn't take away from my beauty but only added to it. I decided to embrace my scar and allow it to be a part of who I am, and I have never covered it since.

I began to get recognized in my field as a yoga teacher and as I started to appear on magazine covers, I always requested that they leave my eyebrow as it is. I want to send out a message to women that we should celebrate ourselves just as we are – not in spite of our unique characteristics, but because of them.

XXX Seane

P.O. BOX 1425 · TOPANGA, CA 90290

SEANE@SEANECORN.COM

Anything unique about you that you're inspired to maybe take another look at, or perhaps embrace a little differently—or dare I say fall in love with? Remember, the girl in the mirror can't respond with words of encouragement unless we give her a little love and inspiration.

I learned to love my eyes, which are two different colors!

I feel like I can't help but compare myself to all the gorgeous girls around me.

They're all so much skinnier and prettier and smarter and just... better than I am!

How do I deal with this?

OWWW . . . this one is a killer!

Nothing triggers those painful insecurities faster than comparing ourselves to someone we hold in our minds as better . . . or worse than that, who we think is "perfect." We all have our own version of what perfect looks like: skinny, pretty, athletic, popular, curvy, wealthy. . . . But the one thing we all seem to have in common is how we feel when we see someone who embodies our ideal. Within seconds we can feel reduced to nothing and want to run, hide, disappear—anything not to have to face the pain of feeling like we don't measure up.

How can we trust that we are enough just the way we are? How can we stay confident within ourselves when all around us, it seems like there are other girls that are so much . . . well, better?

↑ The key words there being "seems like"

The Negative Thought Spiral (aka "the Swirl")
She looks amazing...
I look ugly next o her...
Her legs are perfect...
I'll never be as good as her...
Why can't I be more like her?...
I look ugly next o her...
She looks amazing...

How many times have you asked yourself, *What's wrong with me that I don't have that body . . . boyfriend . . . family . . . grade . . . purse . . . car?* Thoughts like these that bombard us one after another are what I call "the swirl." You know, those nonstop negative thoughts that go around and around in our heads and feel like they are sucking us down into the vortex of jealousy, intimidation, and "I'm not good enough."

"I feel like I can't help but compare myself to all the gorgeous girls around me. They're all so much skinnier and prettier and smarter and just . . . better than I am! How do I deal with this?"

Hello
my name is
"Miss I nsecure"

There was this girl who whenever I was around her, I'd immediately feel like a big loser. To me, she was the ultimate in every way--looks, success, the whole package. She represented to me a level of everything I felt I didn't have, and everything I wanted to be. I remember one night I was having dinner with a group of great friends at a restaurant we all love. We were having an amazing time, laughing and just loving life--until I looked up and there she was. It was like my life force was zapped instantaneously.

As she was walking toward me with a big smile to give me a hug hello, the swirl began in my head: "Ugh! She's so pretty....She has the career I want.... I can't compete.... Everybody loves her...." Suddenly, I was Miss Insecure. Amazing how right in the middle of a purely joyful moment, I allowed her mere presence to make me feel reduced, right? Within seconds I went from loving my life to focusing on all the things I felt were missing from it that I assumed she must have. --XOE

No one knew of course, that this whole thing was playing out in my head.

Let's get real: everyone deals with worrying about not measuring up to other girls in one way or another...

Girls Share Their FEELINGS OF BEING "LESS THAN"

From: < Joselyn >

To: < elizabeth@ask-elizabeth.com >

This is probably a little shallow to say but when I am around my REALLY pretty/gorgeous friends my inner critic is so loud! If I'm hanging with them I spend hours getting ready, I want to measure up. I want them to feel like I am on their level when they hang with me. It's also pretty embarrassing when you're hanging out with someone really pretty and guys constantly hit on them and don't even see you. You at least want to get SOME attention. —Joselyn,16

even see you. You at least want to

From: < Alisha >

To: < elizabeth@ask-elizabeth.c

I actually get jealous of other girls' voices. For a long time when I first came to this school, kids would say I sounded white.... They would make fun of me, call me an Oreo...say, 'Oh you're so bougie.' It makes me wish I sounded like everyone else here. —Alisha, 14

From: < Maya >

To: < elizabeth@ask-elizabet

I'll be at Disneyland, or Walmart, or school, and I'll pretty much analyze every girl I see to see which parts of them I like better than mine. Like if their arms are nicer, if they have my dream legs, if their boobs are better, if they have a better sense of fashion.... —Maya, 15

When I get dressed in the locker room for gym, I secretly look around to see what other girls look like naked so I can see how I compare.

—Christina, 16

I'm embarrassed to admit this, but I often feel jealous of my mom for being skinnier than me. Whenever we do exercise classes together, I always feel mortified that she's in better shape than I am.

Frances, 16

To: < elizabeth@ask-elizabeth.com >

I live near a rich population, and when I see girls wearing the new style of clothes, I can't help but envy them because I can't afford to buy that stuff. I walk through the hallways of my high school and can't help but feel ashamed of how I look or how I'm dressed. —Regina, 17

There is a girl in my English class with a 4.0 averdge who just always knows what's going on in our work. The hard work I have to do to even come close to being how good she is... It's insane. It makes me feel like a stupid idiot compared to her. -Katie, 17

To: < elizabeth@ask-elizabeth.com >

It can be a bit disheartening when you're shopping with your friends and one of them asks the store clerk if they carry a size zero; meanwhile, you're going through the racks to find the only size ten. Yeah, eventually it does do a number on your self-esteem. —Sophie, 16

"I feel like I can't help but compare myself to all the gorgeous girls around me. They're all so much skinnier and prettier and smarter and just . . . better than I am! How do I deal with this?"

The "Gift" of Jealousy

I know what you're thinking. . . . *Elizabeth, how can feeling jealous be a "gift"?* But don't worry, I'll explain.

Whenever we're faced with any feeling or situation that causes us pain, we have two choices: we can let it take us down, or we can look at it as an opportunity to grow. Even though it hurts like crazy, it can make us take a look at ourselves in a way we might not have before, and can show us what we're made of. That's true empowerment—and that's why I call it a gift.

→Not just comparison moments-I mean any challenge in life.

ELIZABETH BERKLEY

Let me tell you a little story....

Dance has always been my biggest love. In many ways, it has shaped my life. It was definitely the first thing I felt good at; it's when I dance that I feel most free and not in my head. My parents took my dream to be a performer seriously, so when I was thirteen they brought me from my hometown in Michigan to L.A. to spend the summer in Jackie Sleight's class--the best in Hollywood. And that's where Molly Brecker entered my life.

NO "swirling" when I'm dancing... only twirling. Ha! ☺

Molly was two years older than me and assisted Jackie. I was in awe and wanted to have everything she had: her dance outfits, her hair, her body, not to mention her talent. When we would learn a combination, my eyes were glued to her to see how much faster she was picking it up. Grrr--it seemed effortless for her! During every combination we did, she seemed stronger and sharper than

me. I was getting so down on myself that I only wanted to take classes that I knew she didn't take. For the first time I seriously worried about whether I had what it took to make it in this business if there were other Molly Breckers out there.

Of course I fantasized that Molly had the perfect life to go along with all her seemingly perfect attributes. One day I heard that her dad had passed away when she was a young girl. Hearing about her life and what she had overcome humanized her to me; my heart went out to her. My mom always told me that when you're jealous of someone, you can't focus just on one quality she has, and my mom was right; I realized that there was much more to the story than what I saw on the surface.

"I feel like I can't help but compare myself to all the gorgeous girls around me. They're all so much skinnier and prettier and smarter and just . . . better than I am! How do I deal with this?"

There wasn't an actual dramatic moment that stopped me from doing this jealousy madness; I honestly just eventually got fed up with being mean to myself. It was like, "Wait a minute.... How much longer are you going to stop yourself from enjoying the thing you love just because you think someone else might look or be better? No way. Enough of that!" I saw that it was me, not Molly, who was blocking the joy I got from dancing--the thing that I love to do more than anything on the planet. Here I had this dream opportunity and I didn't want to let it pass me by. → BTW, Molly was always only a complete sweetheart to me...

I realized that it was time to take that pain and fear and turn it into something else: drive. I started looking at Molly as inspiration. If I loved how she did a routine, I would take what I liked and try it in my own style. It made me push myself to another level instead of defeating me. I'm not going to lie.... There were still moments in class when the negative thoughts and jealousy would creep back in, but when it would happen, I was able to feel it, acknowledge it and let it pass rather than get caught up in "the swirl." Even though I felt Molly was technically a better dancer, I discovered that my passion and individual style made my dancing unique. Interesting how while I was wanting all that time to be someone else, I actually found myself. Thank you, Molly Brecker, wherever you are! --XOE

The daily suffering I felt inside was my own doing.

I actually asked her for tips that made my turns better!

I want to be ~~her~~! Myself! ♡

Me at 12

ACTION STEPS: Stop the Swirl

Okay, so what do you do when your own version of Molly Brecker (or "restaurant girl") shows up, or whatever or whoever else it is who makes you want to crawl into a hole and hide? How can you prevent one negative thought from creating a full-blown swirl of *I'm nothing . . . not good enough . . . a complete loser*?

Here are some thoughts on what to do when you realize it's happening . . . some from me, and some from other girls who have faced the swirl (and escaped!).

ACTION STEP # 1

Remember That No One's Life Is Perfect

"I'd be so happy if I could just have her ______."

"Everything would be so much better if only I had her ______."

"All of my problems would go away if I had her ______."

Fill in the blanks, baby! Whatever fantasy you've made up about how someone's life is better than yours, I can promise you that no one's life is perfect just because she has amazing legs, lives in a big house, is a star athlete or a straight-A student, or even is a celebrity. Just like I didn't know the truth about Molly Brecker, you never know what goes on in someone's private life or in her mind. So the next time you find yourself idealizing someone else, remember that you're seeing only one piece of the puzzle.

ACTION STEP # 2

Reclaim Your Power

If you think about it, a lot of this comparison thing comes down to fear that we aren't good enough, or that our "status" in some way will be threatened by someone who is—God forbid—better. We lose sight of our own worth (and happiness) because we become so obsessed with how we measure up against someone else, instead of staying focused on our personal best, just like I did

"I feel like I can't help but compare myself to all the gorgeous girls around me. They're all so much skinnier and prettier and smarter and just . . . better than I am! How do I deal with this?"

when I saw the girl in the restaurant. In that moment, I didn't even consider anything that I might be proud of that I have accomplished; as far as I was concerned, her accomplishments canceled mine out.

So how about we get your focus back on you and your individual qualities, talents, interests, and dreams, and not on anyone else's? I love what seventeen-year-old Tia said about this: "Girls in general . . . our bad habit is that when we see someone really pretty, we automatically build them up and put ourselves down. That's why we don't see ourselves as beautiful—we're training our eyes the wrong way."

So true!

Remember in the question "What do you do when you look in the mirror and hate what you see?" how you retrained yourself to look for what you like about your appearance? Well, now it's time to take a good look at and truly own what's special about who you are on the *inside*.

≡ As in: claim and completely hold as yours

What are your gifts, strengths, and talents that set you apart as the special creature you are? Are you a great athlete, an amazing friend, a great cook? Are you smart, talented, creative, funny? Focusing on those things is the perfect way to train your eyes back in the right direction, as Tia said. No more wasting time and opportunities dwelling on what makes someone else shine!

ACTION STEP # 3

Be Generous in Your Thoughts About Someone Else

I always wonder why we think there can be only *one* pretty girl, *one* top student, *one* star, *one* star athlete. Why, exactly, does everything have to be a competition? That just makes us feel jealous and puts us automatically into comparison and better than/worse than mode. What if we actually could see what is great and special about another girl, knowing it doesn't take away from what's amazing about us?

You know that girl you're most jealous of? C'mon, give her a compliment, either in your mind or right to her face. Don't worry, you're not robbing yourself of what makes you special. Nothing about her has the power to delete you. My acknowledging that Molly Brecker was a great dancer didn't mean I wasn't talented in my own way. Two girls in a given room can be equally special. You can both stand in all your beauty and intelligence and talent without diminishing the other, and actually you both end up winning.

ELIZABETH BERKLEY

A few years ago, I was cast in a Broadway play that was a huge hit. The play had been running for a few months already when the director called me to quickly jump in to replace one of the female leads. So when I came on board, there was already a cast of actors who were closely bonded, and I felt like the new girl in school. I'd never met the actress (Parker Posey) who was playing the other female lead, and I prayed I wouldn't encounter any of that girl-competition stuff that can be so common.

→ I had to learn the role in three days... Yikes!

My first day I was beyond nervous. When I got to the theater, the stage manager showed me to the dressing room I would be sharing with Parker. I was so surprised to find that she had put flowers on my makeup table and wrote a big note in red lipstick on my mirror, saying, "Welcome to your new home!" So sweet, right?

This warm welcome felt like a big hug. If she had set up a competitive, weird energy from the start, it would have been so sad to share that space and work together... not to mention what we both would have missed out on in terms of the amazing friendship we still have. We both ended up winning because of her generosity. I'll always be grateful to her for showing me that there are girls who aren't afraid to share the spotlight. --XOE

me ↙

→ Parker

PLAYBILL®

WWW.PLAYBILL.COM

It's a beautiful (and very liberating) thing to let someone else shine without feeling like it takes away anything from you. No joke, the more you appreciate what makes someone else amazing, the more your own light shines, because you'll feel that spirit of generosity from within. The world is an abundant place, and there's enough for everyone.

Here's how sixteen-year-old Tara put it:

I try to tell everyone—girl, boy, dog, cat—that they look great or I love their hair, shoes, etc, (not in a fake way). Karma is a cool thing. If you're confident, and compliment others and acknowledge the beauty in others, you will receive the same. There's a certain glow to people who do this.

"Who's the Fairest of Them All?"

Here's what it comes down to:
in all the world, in all of time,
there will never be another girl like you.

No one will ever have your same story,
gifts, strengths, hopes, and dreams.

No one will ever take the risks you take, learn the
lessons you learn, feel the pain you feel,
experience the same joys and triumphs.

So when it comes to who's the "best,"
remember that since no one can do you
better than you, no one can compare.

LOVE
32 USA
FIRST-CLASS
USA
he loves me he loves me not
i love him
i love him not
LOVE
29 USA
i love him i love him
i love him i love him i love him
i love him...
i love him not
LOVE

2
and Loss

FINDING YOUR WAY THROUGH MATTERS OF THE HEART

* *

* Love relationships can be some of the most beautiful experiences in life, and they can also be the most challenging—and confusing. There's flirting, dating, falling in love, breaking up, and everything in between...it's a lot for one girl to figure out on her own!

But don't worry, that's what we're all here to help you with. Here you'll get to peek into other girls' private experiences and hear their secrets, thoughts, ideas, and advice to help support you in all things love-related, along with some things I want to share with you from my own heart. The goal is to empower you to choose and create relationships that make you genuinely happy. Yes, it really is possible!

Before we jump in, I just want to let you know that throughout this chapter, you'll see that I use the words "he" and "guy." I know that some of you are in romantic relationships with other girls. Please know that I fully honor, accept, and love every single one of you, whomever you love. I use the male references simply for ease in reading so it won't get annoying to keep seeing he/she, him/her...you get it.

And now to the heart of the matter (ha!).

How do you get a guy to know you're alive?

Let's say you're at a party. Standing on the other side of the room is the guy from your English class who you are massively crushing on. He's over there, talking and laughing with his friends, and you're over here, not sure he even knows you exist. What do you do? Are you one of the bold ones who could casually walk over to him and start talking? Or are you like the girl who asked this question and the thousands more like her who think, *How could I possibly ever get this guy to notice me—let alone like me?*

Attracting someone can definitely seem like an intimidating game with its own set of complicated rules: playing hard to get, planning your approach, flirting, making the right moves. And yes, I'm not going to lie—there is an element of strategy to it! But I promise, there are ways to actually remove the fear and have fun getting that guy to notice what an amazing girl you are.

What Not to Do

I know, it's weird that I'm starting with what not to do, right? But before I spill all the juicy secrets about how to get a guy's attention, I want to talk for a second about something that doesn't serve us: *being fake.* You know, pretending to be something or someone you're not just to get a guy. We've almost all done it, and it inevitably backfires.

ELIZABETH BERKLEY

There was a time in my life when I was very good at being what I thought other people wanted. Having a guy like me (or not) could make or break my confidence, so I would focus entirely on delivering his "dream girl." I was so intent on making sure this guy wanted me that I never even bothered to consider if he was someone that I actually wanted, or whether or not he deserved me.

So for a little while, when it came to dating, I got stuck in a pattern of trying to be whatever I thought each guy liked. Either I would try to emulate the look or style of the types of girls they previously dated or I would try to

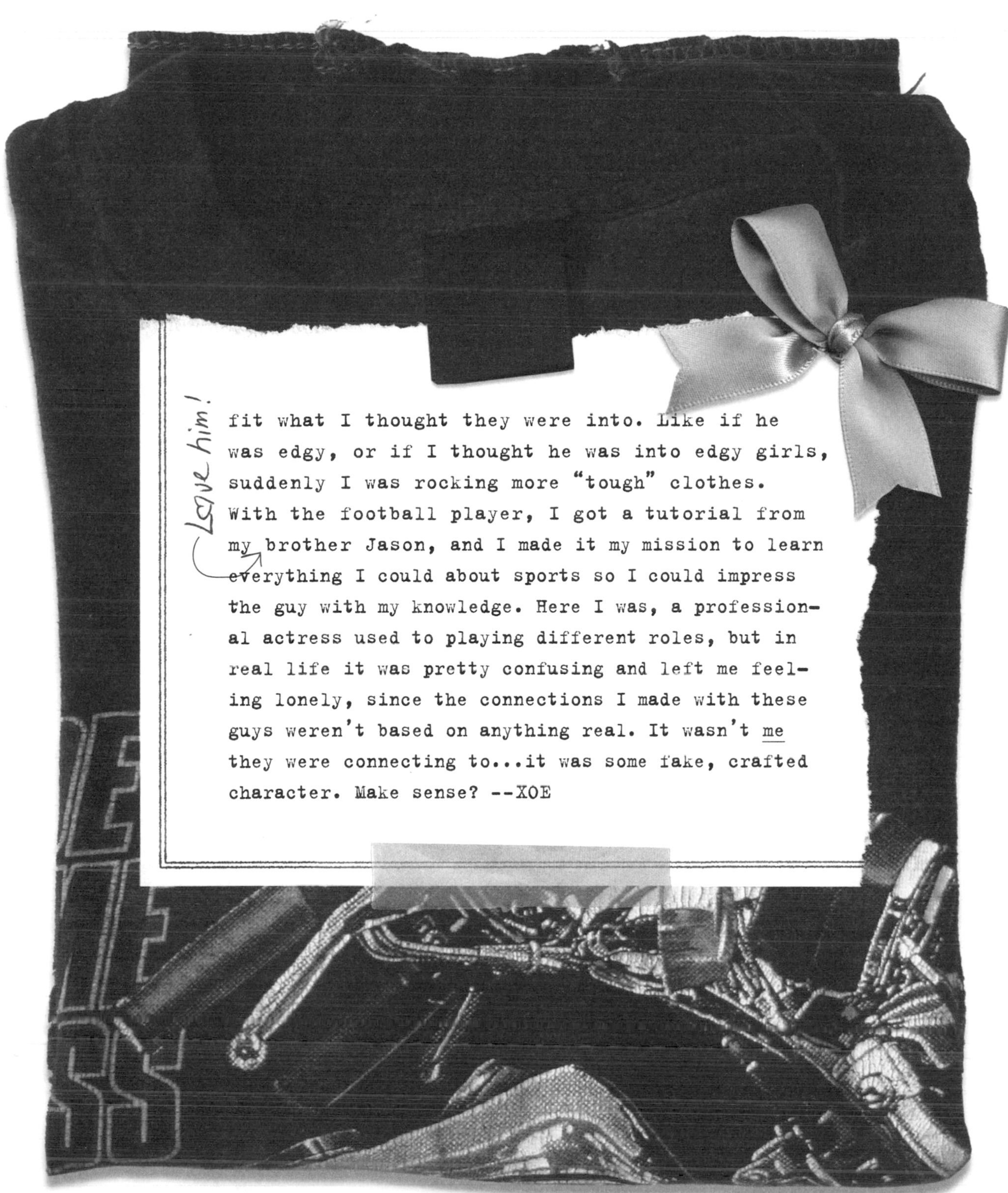

fit what I thought they were into. Like if he was edgy, or if I thought he was into edgy girls, suddenly I was rocking more "tough" clothes. With the football player, I got a tutorial from my brother Jason, and I made it my mission to learn everything I could about sports so I could impress the guy with my knowledge. Here I was, a professional actress used to playing different roles, but in real life it was pretty confusing and left me feeling lonely, since the connections I made with these guys weren't based on anything real. It wasn't me they were connecting to...it was some fake, crafted character. Make sense? --XOE

Showing the Real You

It can be scary to put ourselves out there and risk being rejected. When you show up as who you authentically are and someone doesn't respond the way you want them to, it feels more personal for sure. But the problem with creating a façade is that even if you do end up getting the guy's attention with that persona you've created, you're stuck having to be that fake person . . . *all the time.* And how exhausting does that sound?

ELIZABETH BERKLEY

I once had my eye on this cute guy. I met him on a night when I was in a bit more of a glam mode, and since that was the night I got his attention, I decided that I needed to maintain that look at all times. This wasn't something he was telling me he preferred; it was just an assumption I made that he preferred the "glam Elizabeth," and I was afraid I'd disappoint him if I showed him the real me without any makeup. I'll be honest: I didn't believe I was pretty enough without the "mask."

Obviously I wasn't rocking stilettos at the grocery store—ha!

One day, he surprised me by picking me up after a dance class. While that was sweet, I was secretly panicked because, trust me, after a two-hour class, there was no makeup left on this face! It had washed away from all the sweat, and I was left with "au naturel Elizabeth"--raw, real, and no way to hide. I was tempted to run to the bathroom and quickly put makeup on, but I knew that would be ridiculous since he had already seen me.

Guess what? When we got in the car, he told me he loved seeing my face without all that makeup and that my naturalness was more attractive to him. I didn't believe him at first, because I hadn't learned to trust that I was enough just as I was. So I decided to run an experiment, and I showed up for our next date with more natural-looking makeup. It was such a relief to discover that he actually did prefer it. Can you imagine all the energy and time I saved getting ready after that?
--XOE

Not to mention the money I saved on makeup!

Even though it might sound like some lame poster in your guidance counselor's office, it really is true that if you want a guy to notice you, the single most attractive thing you can do is *be yourself.* As sixteen-year-old Melissa said, "I've learned that guys don't necessarily like the girl with the prettiest face or even the best body. Guys like girls who are real, and who they can be themselves around." When you relax and radiate an inner comfort with yourself, it energetically has an effect and the right guys will be drawn to you almost like magic.

Dress Hot or Not

I know I promised the secrets of attraction, but just hang in there with me for one more second, okay? A lot of you have talked about the pressure you feel to dress over-the-top sexy as a way to get guys' attention. We might see a lot of girls doing that, so we feel like that's what we need to do. But I think an important question to ask yourselves is: Who are you dressing like this for—and why? And even more than that, is it the kind of attention you truly want? I'm not judging you—I just want you to consciously be the boss of your own choices!

I went through a phase when I was in my late teens where every outfit I owned was revealing in some way or another. OMG, no joke, when I see pictures from that time, I'm like, "Wow... Couldn't you have picked just one part of your body to expose? Did you really have to flaunt everything at once?" I might as well have been wearing a sign that said, "Hey, look at me! I'm sexy.... Please see me that way!"

Looking back, I understand that I was coming from a place of needing to be seen and validated. Part of my journey was about finding my confidence and expressing myself through outfits with this new body of mine, since I was such a late bloomer and was suddenly getting attention from older guys. Of course we all want to feel attractive and know we're desired. Please, there's no way to shut that off entirely! But there's a way to remove the need that's behind it. And that's what I slowly started to work on, giving myself the validation so I wouldn't need it from any external source. It goes back to a lot of the tools from chapter one. The techniques we talked about there are all good ways to build inner strength that you can carry into every other area of your life.

Now it's my choice if I want to play with different looks in my daily life, not an unconscious need. I love to play with makeup, and I do like to dress sexy sometimes--not trashy but just in a way that feels good to me. Sometimes it's jeans and a T-shirt, or a pencil skirt and high heels--whatever feels intuitively right for that day and is appropriate for where I'm going.

We're girls... We're allowed to have fun and play with our image!

Ultimately, "sexy" is about confidence--feeling good in your mind, body, and clothes no matter what you're wearing. I like how sixteen-year-old Ann Marie put it: "Girls in my school come in wearing a tank top and PJ bottoms, but because they're confident, it looks so sexy. And that rocks. I've seen other girls come in with skinny jeans, heels, makeup, the whole thing, but because they're not rocking the confidence, it doesn't work. It's not about what you wear.... It's about how you carry it."

Back when I was dressing in very revealing ways and putting all that pressure on myself to live up to a preconceived idea I had of what "sexy" was, I wish I had really gotten that I didn't need to do all that for someone to be attracted to me. And so that's what I want to pass along to you, from one girl to another. You are beautiful and sexy when you are just being YOU... regardless of whether you're dressed "hot" or not. --XOE

Attraction 101

Okay, I promised you I'd pass along the tips and tricks from other girls about how to get a guy's attention, and here they are! Every girl has her own unique vibe and style, but hopefully these girls will give you some ideas that you can take and make your own.

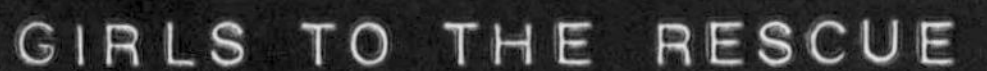

HI THERE!

Hello!

Hi Cutie!

How We GET THAT GUY TO KNOW WE'RE ALIVE

From: < Beth >

To: < elizabeth@ask-elizabeth.c

Subject: know we're alive

I would say the most important thing when you finally start talking to someone you're into is just to be natural.... Just keep it simple and talk about basic stuff, like, 'Hey, what'd you think of that math test? Are you going to that party this weekend?'...anything like that, to make him feel at ease. Even just a simple 'Hey, how's it going?' can go a long way.
—Beth, 15

Don't forget, they get nervous too!

Hi, there!

i think people are attracted to happiness. i'm not saying this casually— I worked really hard to get happy within myself. One time i went to a party and saw this guy who i thought was one of the most beautiful people in the world. i was just walking around, feeling upbeat, and so i kind of naturally started talking to him, and he responded. it felt easy because it was just an extension of my mood. —Stevie, 18

How's it going?

If I like a guy that I know, I'll just send him a text, like, "Hey, what's up? How are you?" Just to get a casual dialogue going. ~ Molly, 17

To: < elizabeth@ask-elizabeth.com >

Subject: Get That Guy to Know We're Alive

One way to begin pushing yourself out of hanging back is to make a checklist of things you want to say or do in approaching the guy you like. First maybe it's just saying hi. Then maybe you IM him, or text him. Then the next time you meet up maybe you hug him hello, then maybe you casually ask him if he wants to hang out One step at a time makes it feel less overwhelming. —Alex, 16

When it comes to guys I like, I usually have my guy friend put it out there, like say, "Ariel is really hot, isn't she?" And if the guy agrees, I'll start talking to him. For me, it helps to know that it's safe before I make any aggressive move. Ariel, 16

What I think also works well is the simplicity of a warm smile (which can give him the sign that you're approachable); subtle eye contact can also give him that cue and "permission" to connect (especially if you're flirting from across a room. It's like saying, "It's okay, you can come on over."). Then once you start talking, you can ask him genuine questions about himself. That takes the pressure off you. Plus, showing interest in someone is very alluring to the other person. Don't you feel special when someone wants to know more about you? Before I send you out there to put any of this into practice, though, I have to ask: Does this guy even deserve your attention? If the answer is yes, then of course go for it. If not, save your magic for the one who gets you.

As girls, remember that we have way more power than we realize—own it and enjoy it!

How do you know if you're in the right relationship?

You'd think it would be easy to know whether someone is right for us, wouldn't you? But in matters of the heart, things aren't always that black-and-white. Sometimes it's flat-out obvious, but it can also be confusing and take experience and time and, yes, sometimes pain, to figure out if this is the right person for you.

No matter what the outcome, every relationship we're in gives us another opportunity to discover what does and doesn't work for us. It's kind of fun to think of it as a treasure hunt, where each step leads us closer to the gold. Each person we love—or even like—reveals a little more to us about what we want and need.

I'm not going to sit here and tell you what kind of relationship you should be in or who you should be with. If someone did that to me, I would be so bugged! I know that's something personal for every one of us. But what I can do is help you figure out if you're in something that is best for *you.*

Choosing What You Want

Picture an orchard full of trees with apples just waiting to be picked. So many of us allow ourselves to be like those apples—just hanging out, waiting for a guy to come along and choose us. Think about it: if you're going to devote your precious time and energy to someone, they'd better be worth opening your heart to. We shouldn't just wait to be picked by just anyone!

A lot of us might feel so happy to know that someone likes us that we don't stop to even think if we like them back or if this is even the right person for us. But we actually do have a choice about who we want to be with. I'm not saying let's all start suddenly asking guys out (ha!), but remember that we're not powerless here.

So what I want to give you are some of the signs of a healthy relationship, so you can check in with yourself to know if your relationship is a keeper. You know how a BFF would ask you tons of questions to make sure you're in the kind of good relationship you deserve? Well, you'll act like her, only this time you'll be asking the questions of yourself.

POSITIVE SIGN №1

There Is More Joy Than Struggle

Being happy means that you can trust someone with anything... that you smile at the thought of him... that you know deep down he has your best interests at heart. Those are the things I look for that tell me I've got something good going.

—Tess, 17

Sounds obvious, right? But you'd be surprised how many girls settle for "kind of happy," and I don't want you to ever settle in your relationships. A relationship is supposed to add joy, inspiration, wisdom, and all those good things to your life—not stress you out or make you miserable. If it's constantly dragging you down, trust me, you are better off on your own.

I'm not saying that every relationship is perfect and balanced one hundred percent of the time. Every couple has their ups and downs. There are always going to be challenging times, and times when one person's needs are greater than the other's. As seventeen-year-old Hope wisely said, "I feel like people think a good relationship is going to be perfect all the time, but that's not true. I think the good just has to outweigh the bad . . . by a lot, though."

Overall, do you feel energized and empowered by this relationship, or depleted and diminished by it? Do you wake up excited at the thought that this person is in your life, or worried about whatever drama the day is going to bring? Are there extreme highs and lows, or is there a nice consistency and a sense of peace in your heart?

We'll talk about all of these things in the next few pages, but I think it's good from the get-go to ask yourself honestly: *Am I happy?*

Hint: true happiness never feels forced.

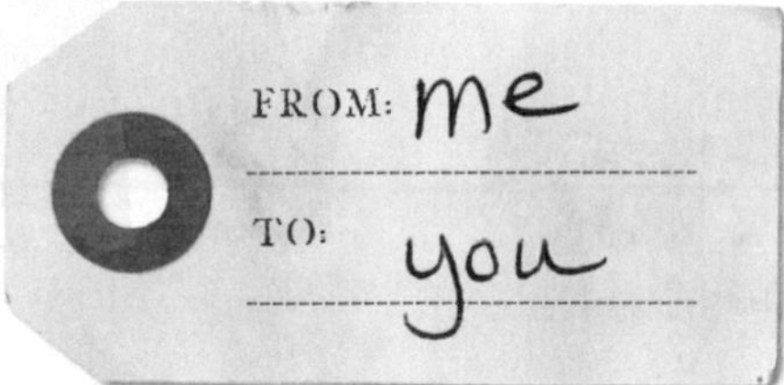

A QUICK NOTE ABOUT SEEKING HAPPINESS...

Of course we want the one we love to make us light up on the inside and feel adored. At the same time, we have to remember that it's never anyone else's job to make up for our own lack of happiness in other areas of our life. They can tell you nice things to boost your self-esteem or to provide encouragement, but if you're always looking to them for that, it's just a Band-Aid--not to mention a LOT of pressure on the other person. It's your job to make yourself stronger from within, and then you can actually create happiness with them from a place of strength, not need. XO E

I LOVE HIM

POSITIVE SIGN #2

You Can Be Yourself with Him

I feel like a HEALTHY RELATIONSHIP is when you LOVE someone despite their FLAWS and COMPLEMENT each other in such a way that YOU are BETTERED just by being in their PRESENCE. –andrea, 18

I LOVE HIM NOT

If you read the previous question, "How Do You Let a Guy Know You're Alive?," then you know that fully being who you are in all your uniqueness is the biggest turn-on there is. But it's also one of the best ways for you to test if the relation-

Shine, baby, shine!

ship you're in is right. Are you pretending to be something you're not, allowing yourself to be in uncomfortable situations, or panicking over pleasing him? Or are you able to just breathe and be who you truly are?

There is such comfort in being known and fully accepted by someone. Sixteen-year-old Sophia explained what that means for her: "For me, it's a lot about being comfortable enough to be able to act weird. I'm sarcastic and constantly joking—I do dumb voices and goofy dance moves. You know how when you first meet someone you hold back and don't do that kind of stuff? I feel like I must really like someone if I let myself do all that around them. That's the thing that makes a ding go off in my head that says, 'This is working.'"

With my husband, Greg I never have to pretend to be something I'm not. It's such a relief to feel safe enough to just be vulnerable and be myself which might include showing him sides of myself I don't show the rest of the world. He has always really encouraged me to open up that way. Such a gift!
Never settle for less... ♡

I LOVE HIM

And because you are your own rare and precious gift, exactly as you are, I want you to ask yourself: *Am I really, fully being myself in this relationship? Is this person getting the real me?* If he isn't, it's worth thinking about what you're both missing out on.

POSITIVE SIGN №3

You've Kept Your Identity

Being in a relationship shouldn't mean that two people morph into one... It's so much healthier to be two people who love what's different about each other. - Shannon, 18

I LOVE HIM NOT

Have you ever felt like you gave yourself away to someone . . . like the "me" got lost in the "we"?

As girls we can be such nurturers and put ourselves in second position (or third . . . or fourth . . .); we sometimes give ourselves away and forget what matters to us in order to be with someone else. You can make your guy a priority, of course, but there needs to be a balance. It's so important to remember to take care of ourselves, too, and not abandon what makes us who we are and feeds our soul.

So how do we do this? By staying clear about what matters to us and sticking to our other personal commitments. This doesn't have to mean we need to have some big, dramatic talk about it—just make sure you keep doing the things that are important to you, like spending time with your friends, studying, exercising, etc. We show people through our actions that we respect ourselves in a way that they need to as well. You'll be able to give so much more to a relationship when you do this, because you'll feel good about yourself.

We really do teach people how to treat us.

For instance, if your boyfriend asks you out for Friday night but you tell him you can't because you already promised your little sister you'd take her to the movies, you're showing him that you're someone who honors her plans, and going forward, he'll respect that. And no doubt he'll love that you're the type of person he knows he can count on, too.

Sometimes we can get so consumed that we might not even realize how much we've given up just to be with someone, until we wake up and see how out of balance our lives have become. That's exactly what happened to seventeen-year-old Maura. . . .

I LOVE HIM

MAURA'S STORY:

'I felt so consumed'

When I was with **Tim** he was all I thought about, and **I** was all **he** thought about, but it just wasn't healthy. I compromised all the other aspects of my life. Even my **BEST Friend** – my *Wife* – I let my relationship with her slide. I started skipping basketball practice, which up until then had been the single most **IMPORTANT** thing in my life, just so I could hang out with him. He wasn't forcing me to.... **I** made these choices and put him above every other priority in my life.

I would **Lie** and get dressed for practice, pretending I was going so no one would notice. Of course I am responsible for my own actions, but in hindsight I see that if he really cared about me, he wouldn't have let me do that stuff.

Eventually I started to see how damaging it was and realized that I was losing a big part of myself. I eventually fell out of Love with him ... I think it was because I fell out of Love with myself.. I'm seventeen, and I'd been with him since I was fourteen.... It was time to grow and develop and learn, and I realized I didn't need a dude to do that. I needed time just for **Maura**. The relationship was Beautiful for what it was, but it was time to move on.

I LOVE HIM

I LOVE HIM NOT

I LOVE HIM

Guys, let me just say that there's nothing wrong with spending a ton of time together. How great is it that of all the people on this planet, you chose each other? It's amazing when you really think about it like that. But just check in with yourself every now and then to make sure you're doing the things that made you the individual he originally fell for. I promise you it's not selfish to take time for yourself. I totally get it, you're madly in love, but don't forget to give some love to the most important person, too—YOU!

POSITIVE SIGN #4

He Meets Your Needs

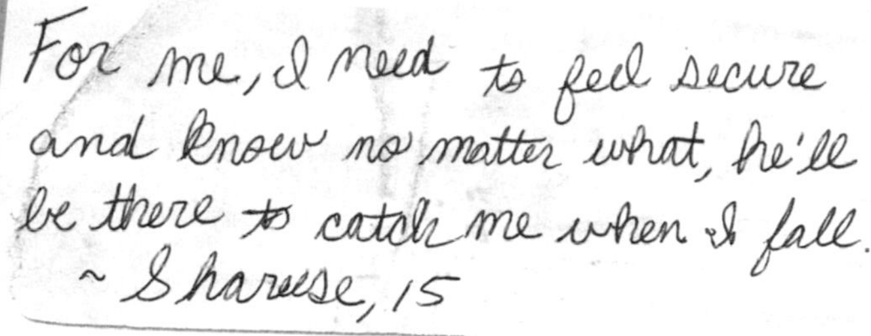

For me, I need to feel secure and know no matter what, he'll be there to catch me when I fall.
~ Sharese, 15

Does he really listen to you when you talk?
Does he make you laugh?
Does he share the same morals and values as you?

What we need in a relationship is personal for each of us, but no matter what, our wants and needs are never wrong. They're just what's true for us. You guys have shared a whole range of different requirements: like eighteen-year-old Ellie, who knows that she'll only be happy with someone who shares her faith; or nineteen-year-old Susanna, who needs someone who she can really open up to and who "gets her"; or fifteen-year-old Maggie, whose bottom-line requirement is that the person has a positive outlook on life ("no tortured souls" is how she put it).

I've learned that in my relationship I need to feel like my guy believes in me and fully supports me in pursuing my dreams. I've had relationships where that wasn't the case, for different reasons: once because it was threatening to the whatever!

guy to have me fearlessly go after my goals, and another time because he → weird, right?
was strangely jealous of my focus and passion for what I do. Remember how I said each step leads you closer to the gold? Well, the pain I felt from not feeling supported by them was like a clue—it was what showed me that support is one thing I absolutely must have in my relationship in order for me to be happy.

For you it might be something completely different, but whatever it is, you know deep down if your relationship needs are being met. And if you don't know what those needs are yet, don't worry, they will get clearer as you experience different relationships. I had to kiss a few frogs before I found my prince. . . . Know what I'm saying?

You Feel Okay Speaking Up When Something's Wrong

Raw truth is what it comes down to for me in a relationship. I need to be able to tell him what's on my mind and have him be okay with that! -Zhane, 18

Of course it would be great if someone would just intuitively know what we're thinking and what we want from them, wouldn't it? But the truth is that sometimes you have to come right out and say when something's bothering you, even though I totally get how hard that can be to do.

Some of you have told me you feel afraid to talk to your guy about something that you wish he would do—or not do. You've shared things like, "I don't want to be annoying" or "I'm scared he'll leave me if I bring up anything I'm not

I LOVE HIM

I LOVE HIM

I LOVE HIM NOT

I LOVE HIM

the best way to get your needs met, btw

comfortable with." Well, forget that! If someone is not okay with you expressing yourself in an honest, loving way, then you are definitely not in the right relationship. Please don't stuff down your feelings for fear someone won't want to be with you! If you respect yourself enough to speak up, you will attract only the kind of guys into your life that will mirror that respect right back to you.

You'll be so happy to see how much better things can be when you let him know what's on your mind. Think about it this way: if there was something you were doing—or not doing—that was standing in the way of your guy feeling happy in your relationship, wouldn't you want him to share that with you so you could have a shot at changing it?

Here are some stories from other girls that will give you some ideas on how to talk to your guy about something that's bugging you. For more about speaking up for yourself, you can also take a look at "If a friend hurts your feelings, how do you confront her without making her mad?" in chapter three.

How to SPEAK YOUR TRUTH TO YOUR GUY

My boyfriend used to constantly look at his phone when we would be out to dinner, which upset me. I didnt want to become passive-aggressive about it, so I said to him in a very normal way that it bothered me when he looked at his phone during dinner because it felt like he had better things to do than be there with me. I didn't get angry at him, I just made it more of a conversation, not accusing him or saying he was a bad person, just saying I didn't like the behavior. This worked really well because he didn't feel like he had to defend himself.

— Jamie, 16

It's so important how you do it — no one wants to feel attacked, right?

SHARE

From: < Zoe >

To: < elizabeth@ask-elizabeth.com >

Subject: Speak Your Truth

I had a debate coach who taught me to say things in a more definitive way. He showed me how not to make my voice go up like a question at the end of a sentence when I am intending to make a statement, because it would always sound like I was asking permission to express myself. *powerful tip!*

For example, instead of saying to my boyfriend, 'I'm sorry, but do you think we could maybe just go out by ourselves tonight.... Would that be okay?' I'd say, 'I'd rather we go out by ourselves tonight instead of with all our friends.' By my expressing myself without being meek or apologizing, he respected my requests more, and we'd actually discuss things instead of getting into some whole weird fight, which happened only because I was holding back my true feelings. —Zoe, 16

Let's all start catching ourselves when we start a sentence with "I'm sorry"—no apologizing for being truthful!

BE DIRECT

For me, it's about being direct. You can just lay it out, you know? Like "This is how it is. This is not how things can rock out... If you're going to be all silent and distant, that's not okay with me," and see what he says. Then you can get the clarity you need and choose to stay with him or not.

Rose, 18

From: < Tina >

To: < elizabeth@ask-elizabeth.com >

Subject: Speaking your truth to a guy

My boyfriend goes to school in another state. It was hard for me to trust him, because we made an agreement that we would call each other when we got home both weekend nights, so I could feel more secure, but he would forget to call a lot. That would leave me really worried and anxious, so I tried talking to him about it, but he kept blowing it off like it wasn't a big deal. Since he wasn't able to see what bothered me about it, I gave him a scenario where we switched roles and he was the one worried sick and freaking out that I was with another boy. He realized my point, and it hasn't happened since. I think letting him see it from my perspective helped him see I wasn't overreacting. —Tina, 18

When I recently had a whole big thing with my boyfriend, I vented through writing on a secret blog that I keep like a diary. The next day, I went back to read what I wrote, made some minor edits, and then shared it with him. I've used this writing technique a few times to communicate, because I know I can lose control in the midst of a big fight. This is how I get the best results when I speak up for myself → in writing!

— Maggie, 16.

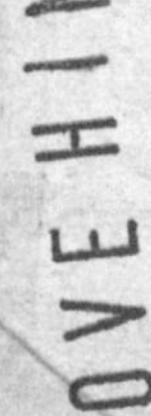

If you've said your truth and he isn't honoring it, then he simply isn't the right one for you. But if he does step up, then I'd say you've got a good one. That's a great sign that you are with an equal partner.

I love what seventeen-year-old Rayna says about this: "Nothing is absolutely perfect in relationships. Arguments happen, and feelings can be hurt even in the most loving circumstances. What sets a healthy relationship apart is having the respect to always listen to what the other person has to say and having the desire to fix small problems as they come. If someone's not willing to do that, who needs them?"

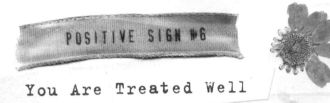

POSITIVE SIGN #6

You Are Treated Well

I think relationships are meant to build you up and improve you as a person, never break you down. — Andrea, 16

I have a friend who always reminds me, "Remember, you're the prize." This isn't about being conceited but just about knowing how incredibly valuable you are, and that you don't ever have to settle for anything less than you deserve.

So many of you have such a hard time believing that you're worth being treated well that you've asked, "What does being treated well look like?" I think seventeen-year-old Audrey expressed so beautifully what it means for her: "When I was in the right relationship it was easy to see. He always treated me like a princess. He told me how he felt about our relationship and always wanted to talk out any issue we had, whether big or small. Whenever he went out with the guys or one of his girlfriends, he always texted me and told me when he got back home safely and where he went. He could tell if I was upset, and if I was, he would comfort me. Basically, he just knew what to do to make me happy and showed me nothing but respect."

Sounds amazing, right? Well, we can all have that—or whatever else we dream of—if we are willing to stay true to what we know we deserve. One of the biggest lessons I think we all learn at one time or another is knowing how you will and won't let people treat you.

If you don't have an example of a good ~~relation~~ relationship in your life, you can create your own great vision.

I LOVE HIM

I LOVE HIM NOT

I LOVE HIM NOT

I once had a relationship that was so filled with daily drama that when I look back, I don't know how I was able to deal with the roller-coaster ride. One day he would be caring and loving, and the next verbally abusing me until I cried. He was really nice to me when I was feeling vulnerable or in a funk, which made me feel like he cared so much, but when I was succeeding or feeling good about myself, he'd put me down or create drama between us just to throw me off. I was so deeply entrenched in our unhealthy dynamic that I actually thought it was my fault if he was in a bad mood. I would wake up not knowing if we'd have a hellish day with me reduced to tears, or whether it would be an "up" day (the ones I stayed around for).

It was so crazy-making, the hold he had over me. I felt like if I left him, then that meant I wasn't strong enough to endure it, or that I was a failure. I didn't want to leave him, since so many people in his life had abandoned him; I loved him and hoped I could change things and make his life better. He warned me from the beginning that he wasn't reliable or solid--I chose to ignore the warning, though, because I thought I could be the girl to "tame" him or "fix" him. Oh, please! Girls, when people tell you who they are, believe them!

Everyone who loved me tried every which way to get me out of this relationship. Ultimately, my godmother said to me that I would get to a point when I would just get tired of the drama and be done once and for all. She was right. He and I ended up going around and around for two years until I finally ended it. --XOE

I've heard so many stories from so many of you who are struggling in an "it's complicated" situation where you feel diminished, disrespected, or even abused. → Or even convinced to do something physical you aren't comfortable with. The drama of those relationships can be exhausting but also addictive and hard to get out of. Maybe you recognize yourself in these stories from girls who've been there, too.

JEN'S STORY: "I overlooked everything because I was in love with him"

I went into my first relationship naïve but anxious to be with Eric, a charming guy who was two years older than me. He had a horrible reputation—drugs, sex, lying, and cheating—but I overlooked it all because I believed him when he said that he wanted to change and leave all that behind. Before even a month had passed, he was telling me that he loved me and there was something different about me. I was in a state of bliss for the next six months. Then one day, out of nowhere, he showed up at my house and callously broke up with me. I crumpled to the floor, crushed. All of my security and self-esteem was tied to our relationship and I couldn't picture my life without him in it.

After a few weeks, I slowly began to heal and move on with my life. He must have sensed this because he called me up, saying that he missed me. I was excited, thinking everything would go back to the way it was. Not quite. Within two weeks he disappeared again. This pattern continued for months. Whenever I started to mend my broken heart, he would lure me back in and then disappoint me again. It hurt so much, but I was so desperate to be with him that I kept going back, like a dog to its master.

Deep down inside I knew he was only messing with me. I'd lost two years of my life to this, and finally one day I called him and asked him definitively if he believed we were meant to be together. He was stoned, so he let his guard slip and said he was only interested in winning me back so I would give him physical affection. Finally something inside of me broke. I would no longer be controlled by his sick little game, and I told him that I was done once and for all.

Sometimes the hardest thing in life is walking away from what you care about most, but after leaving Eric in my past, I found myself happier and at peace with life. And the best thing of all is that I met John, a guy who loves me with all of his heart and never deceives or takes advantage of me. Someone is out there who will treat you better than you could ever imagine, so if you are truly miserable in a relationship, trust me, happiness is just around the corner if you leave the misery behind and go looking for it.

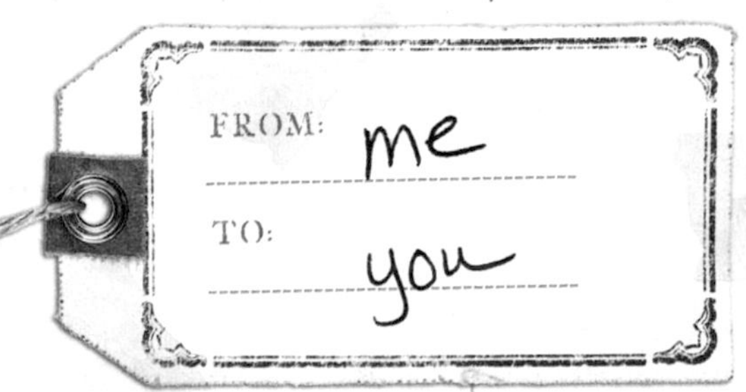

YOU CANNOT FORCE SOMEONE TO CHANGE

So often we think we can save someone and make him become the person we imagine he can be, but the person we need to save here is ourself. It's such a hard lesson, but the reality is that you cannot change someone or make him grow if he is unwilling. When you see that this is who he truly is, you have to ask yourself: "Why am I accepting this as normal? What part of me do I need to heal so I can be strong enough to walk away?" XOE

RACHEL'S STORY:

"The Abuse Turned Physical"

He was perfect... cute, romantic, a football player, popular. But a few months into our relationship, things started to go downhill. He always had to know where I was - at first I thought that it was cute, like, "Aww, that's sweet, my boyfriend always wants to know where I am," but a lot of girls don't realize that it is controlling and sometimes the early stages of emotional abuse, which can lead to physical abuse. I started to get "in trouble" with him if I didn't do things he told me to do, so I started skipping classes and crew practice because he'd make me go be with him. I was in a youth symphony, but I quit because he said it was taking up too much of my time. The first time it happened was at school. He came to class drunk, and slapped my best friend across the face. I hid from him, but when he found me he slammed me up against the lockers and slammed my classroom door on me. I was scared at first, but I convinced myself that it was the alcohol and he never meant to hurt me, so I went back to him.

There's a difference between staying in touch and someone controlling your every move.

The second time was at a party. This time he kicked me, and I flew across the room, hit my head on the wall, and was knocked unconscious. I lay unconscious on the floor for six hours, and woke up with a concussion and two bruised ribs. My "friends" didn't want to call the police because there were drugs and alcohol at the party, and let me lie there convulsing while the party continued.

Once I was able to get up and walk, I went home and told my parents everything. We called the police, and he went to juvenile hall. My house was egged for weeks, and people called me for months, yelling that I could have just broken up with him and ended it there. After speaking with local support networks, I realized that it didn't matter what anyone else thought; my safety was most important. I felt that I needed to stand up for myself and make him understand that he couldn't do that to me.

Since that happend five years ago, I have been speaking out to let other girls realize they deserve better and don't need to put up with it. You need to put your safety and beliefs first.... always.

FROM: ME
TO: you

IF YOU'RE BEING ABUSED

For any of you out there who are in relationships that are abusive--emotionally or physically--I want you to know that there is a way out. If you know in your bones that you are lying to yourself, protecting him by making excuses for his behavior, or blaming yourself over and over, you need help. I know you might feel scared and alone, but please reach out to someone you trust, or turn to one of the resources listed in the Pink Pages on www.ask-elizabeth.com, so you don't have to suffer in this relationship a single second longer. XO E

I LOVE HIM NOT

I LOVE HIM NOT

Ultimately, it comes down to this: too many of us stay in relationships that might not be right for us because he's good to us some of the time, and when it's good, it's great. But someone should treat you well one hundred percent of the time. It's a flat-out requirement. Always remember: you're the prize.

You're in It for the Right Reasons

I think you have to actually like the GUY as much as you like the IDEA of the guy... You know what I mean? – Julia, 15

You don't have to answer this question to anyone but yourself, but in your most private mind, ask yourself: *Why am I with this person?* I think we all know deep down in our hearts if we're with someone because we truly want to be, or for some other reason that feels uncomfortable to admit.

In the relationship I told you about earlier, one of the other reasons I was afraid to leave was that I couldn't stand the idea of someone else coming along after me and loving him; like maybe she had some secret magical power that could fix him, and I would miss out on being with the good version of him. Staying with someone just because you don't want anyone else to have him—*Hmm,* who wins there?

There were a lot of good things in that relationship, and I was also scared that I would never find those things again with someone else. The thing that finally made me leave was realizing that it was not okay to settle out of fear, and that I had to love myself enough to let this go and trust that something better would come along. (And it did!) I like sixteen-year-old Zoe's point: "There can be five things that you love about someone, so you don't want to leave them, but there might be someone else who has another whole five that you love even more . . . or six . . . or seven . . ."

Hey, Zoe, I could have used that advice back then... ha!

I LOVE HIM

I LOVE HIM

I LOVE HIM

So many of us feel such a need to be in a relationship that we'll stay in something even if it isn't serving us, or the other person. Sometimes we do it out of guilt or not wanting to hurt someone. But the bottom line is that if you're not into him, you're not into him—you can't force feelings that aren't there.

Not wanting to be alone is a pretty common motivator. I get this—I really do. It feels comforting to be part of a "we," especially if all your friends have boyfriends. But deep down, we kind of know that we're only giving ourselves a false sense of security this way. It's really important for us girls to learn that it's more than okay to be alone.

Btw, being in something fake can make you feel more alone than if you really were alone

Other times we hang on to someone because he's who we think we're supposed to be with. Maybe he fits the picture of the guy you think is the ideal for you (cute, popular, the same ethnic or cultural background, etc.). But as sixteen-year-old Nadja found, "You can't be with someone just because it fits the picture of what 'type' you or anyone else thinks you should be with. My ex-boyfriend was such a nice guy—our parents were best friends; he was cute and popular and everything I thought I wanted in someone—but honestly, I always knew I was lying to myself. We couldn't talk about real stuff, only surface things. I just knew I didn't want to waste my high school years in a relationship that looked good to everyone else on the outside but felt forced and empty on the inside."

It's not unusual for us to stay in the wrong relationship simply because it's what we know. I know it feels scary to start all over with someone else, but the reality is that staying with someone just because you share a history blocks the possibility of your finding your real dream relationship. And how sad would that be?

When You Know It's Not Right

If you don't see enough of the signs we talked about here in your relationship, you might reach that sad but necessary point of needing to end it. Ugh—no one likes having to break up with someone! Even if we've made the decision in our hearts that it isn't right for us, there are still all these feelings—yours and his—to deal with. It's always complicated.

I wish I could give you a script for the perfect way to say it or do it. . . . if only it was that easy. If you need some support or guidance, some of the stories and thoughts from the girls here might help you figure out how you can end the relationship in a way that honors the relationship for what it was.

How to BREAK UP WITH GRACE

To: <elizabeth@ask-elizabeth.com

You should always be honest and clear with the other person. Never leave room for confusion or uncertainty, because that will only make it harder on them. I think it's good to address with him any issue that made your relationship unsuccessful, and admit any fault that you are accountable for. Don't put everything on the other person. Chances are, the weight of the situation doesn't lie entirely on him. —Eden, 16

My ex was really good to me and made me feel wanted and loved. But I knew it wasn't the right relationship because I wasn't in love with him. I had to tell him I wanted him to be with someone who could give him 150%, and I couldn't do that. He was sad, but he was cool about it. I knew I couldn't keep being so selfish by stringing him along and that this was the right thing to do, even though it sucked. — Michelle, 17

I think timing is important. You don't want to drop it on him right when he's about to go into basketball practice or something. And don't do it at school! Not a good place for that kind of talk. Be smart about it. —Tess, 14

From: < Veronica >

To: < elizabeth@ask-elizabeth.com >

When I was confused about whether to break up with my boyfriend, my dad told me to make a list of all the characteristics I want in a guy, and to check off how many of those he has. It worked, because when I saw it on paper, it was so clear that he had none of those things. So when I went to break up with him, I was honest. I said, 'I think you're a great guy, but you aren't quite the right guy for me. I think we should both give ourselves the chance o find someone who matches what we both need.' He was upset, but how could he argue with that? —Veronica, 16

Listen to Your Heart

I'm going to leave you with some advice from Trina, a very wise eighteen-year-old from Louisiana. Here's what she had to say about knowing whether you're in the right relationship:

I have asked so many people this question—specifically, the ones who are happily married. And they have all said the same thing:

'You just know!'

Umm, okay, that is the most simple, absurd answer I have ever heard... How do you 'just know'? But after I met my boyfriend, Drew, I realized that they were right. So I think you can tell a relationship is right when you smile at the thought of the other person. There isn't anyone you would rather love or be loved by more. You know yourself more than anyone else, so deep down you know if someone is the right person for you, whether or not you want to admit it. Listen to what that voice inside is saying. It'll tell you what you need to know.

How do you
get over
a broken heart?

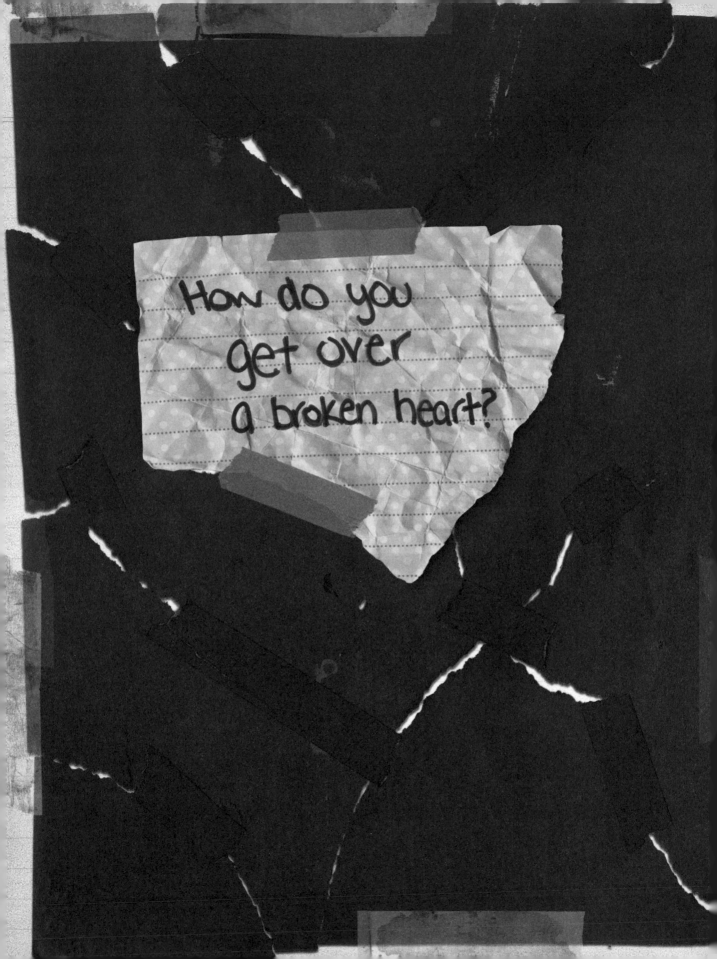

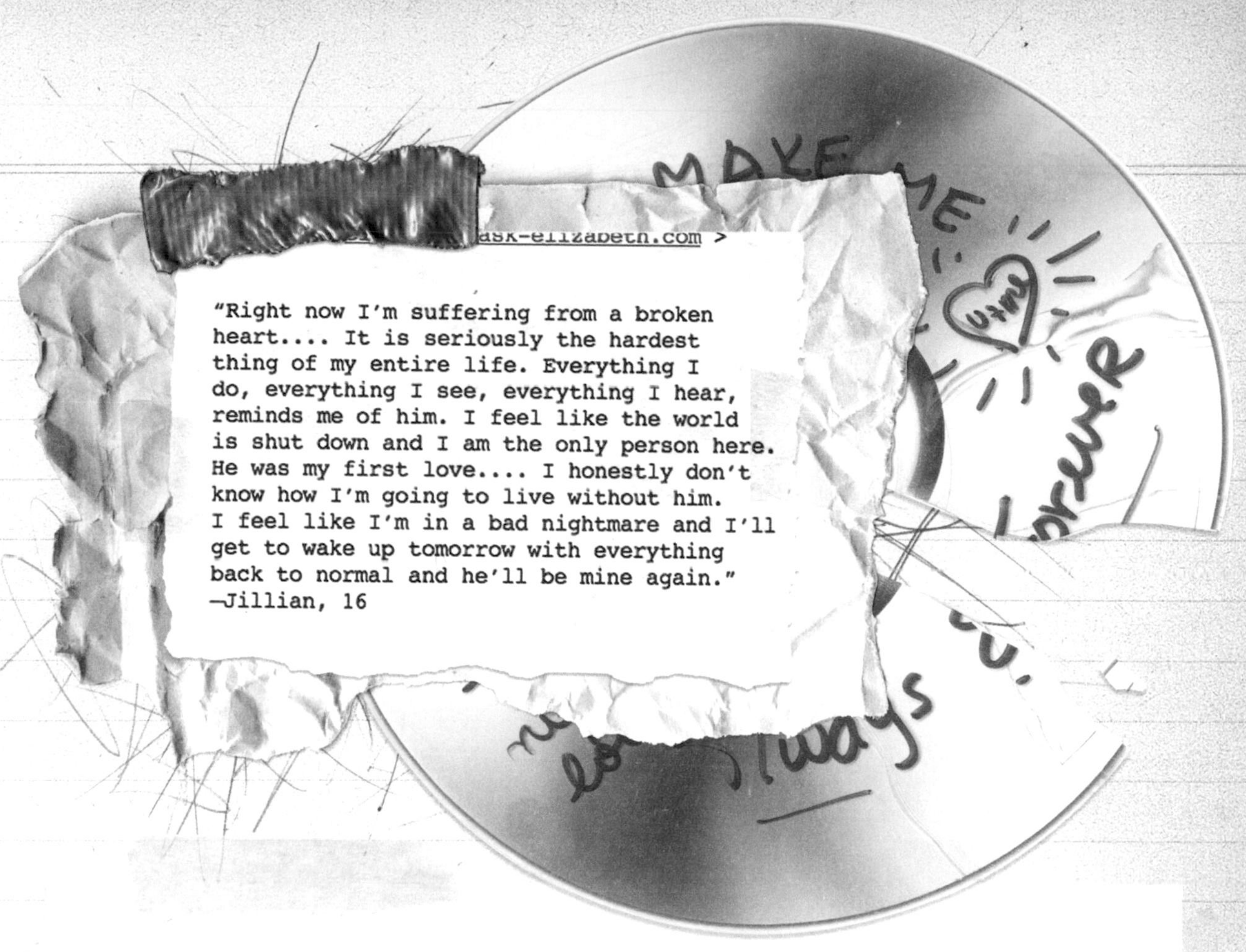

"Right now I'm suffering from a broken heart.... It is seriously the hardest thing of my entire life. Everything I do, everything I see, everything I hear, reminds me of him. I feel like the world is shut down and I am the only person here. He was my first love.... I honestly don't know how I'm going to live without him. I feel like I'm in a bad nightmare and I'll get to wake up tomorrow with everything back to normal and he'll be mine again."
—Jillian, 16

When you're going through this, it can feel like your heart is shattered in a thousand pieces and that nothing and no one (except the one who broke it) can ever make it feel okay again. It's excruciating. Whether someone breaks your heart or it was you that made the difficult decision to end the relationship, the loss can feel like a death of sorts—the grief can be that extreme.

If you break a glass or a vase, you can just throw it in the garbage or try to glue it back together. Your heart? Not so simple. When the question of how to get over a broken heart came up in a workshop in New York City, sixteen-year-old Addie half joked, "Is there really even an answer to that one?" It's true that there's not really one exact answer. But I think that hearing what other girls did to survive and come through to the other side can help you find your way through.

I'll get right to it, because my guess is that if you're experiencing a breakup right now, you're in pain and want help . . . fast!

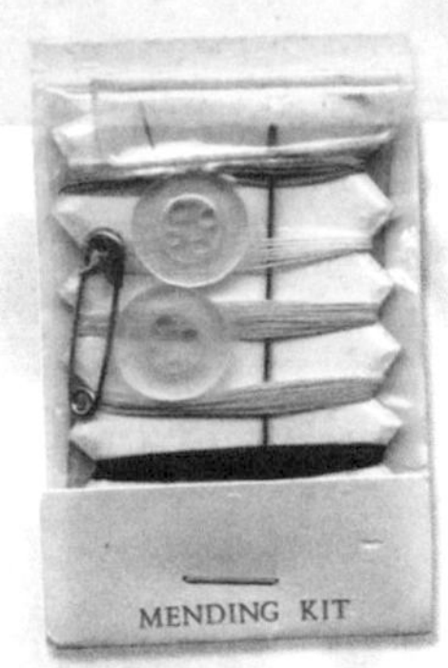

HEALING TOOLS: Caring For Your Wounded Heart

Grief is cyclical, and unfortunately, there's no direct road map to recovery. You might need to come back to some of these tools a few times, in whatever order you need to, as you process the sadness. Just do whatever feels the most natural for you at this moment, and then the next moment, and the next one after that. In time, I promise, you'll come through to the other side.

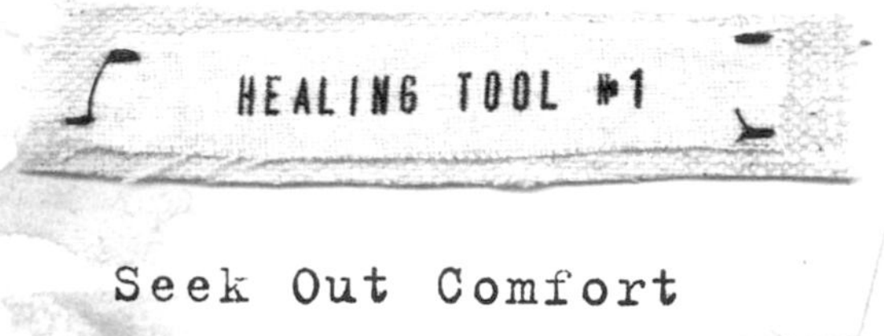

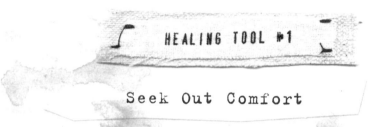

HEALING TOOL #1

Seek Out Comfort

When your heart feels shattered, often the first places you can look to for even temporary solace are the things and people who are most familiar and comforting. When I'm going through something really hard—and trust me, I've been right where you are now—I do the thing I always do when I need to reconnect to myself: I go into the studio and dance. A lighted studio with bare wooden floors is where I always feel the safest. I know I can't dance away the situation, but I can at least find a small pocket of peace to remind me of who I really am in the middle of the storm.

A lot of you have said that listening to music is your immediate go-to. Others meditate, pray, play sports, or go for a walk to clear their thoughts. Seventeen-year-old Hannah puts on her coziest pajamas, curls up on her bed with her dog Max, and has a good cry. She says, "That dog is the best remedy, I swear. . . . I think just feeling that total pure love from a pet can really help when you're hurting." And of course, thank God for amazing friends. As sixteen-year-old Angela said, "Your friends are the best medicine for anything." So whether you need to vent to them or you want to just have some fun to distract yourself for a little while, right now you might need to let your girlfriends be there for you the same way you would be for them. → Nothing wrong with asking for help.

And let's not forget about simple feel-good comforts: ice cream, a funny movie, or even some straight-up pampering. Are these things permanent fixes? No, of course not. But there's nothing wrong with indulging in some pleasures that can give you even a little lift right now. It's okay—it doesn't mean you're running away from the problem; you'll have plenty of chances and time to work through it all. But we all need ways to soothe our souls every now and then.

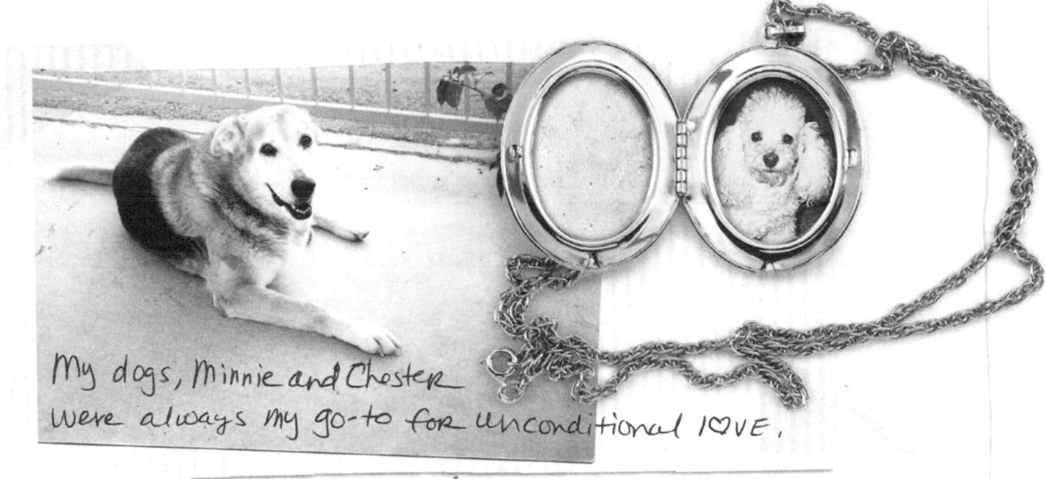

My dogs, Minnie and Chester were always my go-to for unconditional LOVE.

I just want to make sure we're all on the same page: when we're talking about temporary remedies to turn to for comfort here, we're talking about harmless ones, okay? I know some of you who are hurting might feel tempted to seek out dangerous ways to numb the pain—drinking, overeating, drugs, cutting, etc.—but those behaviors are so self-destructive. You're going through enough—you need to give yourself care right now, not punishment and self-loathing! I promise you, these behaviors only create more problems . . . and then there's still the broken heart underneath, waiting to be fixed.

Here's eighteen-year-old Ricki's story about choosing your source of solace wisely....

RICKI'S STORY:

"I went to the dark place"

I had one breakup that was a nightmare. It was a really fast, really intense relationship. I actually left my boyfriend, who was an amazing person, for this guy who I was so drawn to. It was so stupid... He was really pretty, a musician, a drug addict, really flaky. He was bad news and I knew it, but I went for it anyway. And suddenly one day he just ended it without giving me any explanation.

Within Four Hours I started drinking like I never did before. I lost my mind for a few weeks. It was so much drama and destructive behavior on my part... I wanted to hurt him by hurting myself. And of course destroying myself didn't change anything between us, and I ended up having to deal with the effects of what I'd done to my life.

It's taken me a lot of go-arounds to learn that when those feelings of intense anger or sadness come up, the issue is never really him, and the only way to deal with those feelings is to pinpoint what the feeling is linked to in me—what feeling is getting triggered—and then I can focus on working on that. Like is it about not wanting to be alone, which is an issue for me, or needing validation that someone cared about me? And once I pinpoint that, I can have it stop being about him and look within myself for what I need to work on.

Looking back, I see that I'd given him all the power. I made my entire life about him, so of course when he withdrew that's when I turned right to hurting myself. The way I ended up getting over that whole thing was getting better myself. I had to rebuild my life, and doing that helped me look at why I'd gotten involved in a relationship like that in the first place.

Let Yourself Feel the Pain

I'm sending you a huge hug right now.

I know you want to do anything you can to numb the pain, make it go away. And even though there are ways to give yourself comfort and relief, those are just momentary bursts of help along the way to real healing. Almost always, the only way out of heartbreak is straight through it.

Here's nineteen-year-old Bethany's tough-love take on it: "Once you've done all the fantasizing and distracting yourself and praying that you will get back together, walk into the bathroom, look in the mirror, and tell yourself straight-out that you're only hiding from what you know you need to do. I will be honest—it freakin' hurts to get your heart broken, but my advice is *let it hurt.* Let it hurt real good, because you need to feel it completely in order to get over it. After a while, you'll be done with the pain and you'll pick yourself up and move on. But it'll be clean."

Please don't put pressure on yourself to just get over it fast. After all, since the relationship meant something special to you, it will be a process. I've learned for myself that if you let yourself feel everything that comes up, instead of rushing through or resisting it, the pain will pass more quickly.

No judging whatever feelings come up for you... they're all real and valid.

Elizabeth Berkley

I once had a relationship that was really beautiful for a long time, but gradually we both changed and grew apart. Even though I knew breaking up was the right thing to do so that we could part before we ended up hating each other, it killed me. He was my first love, so it was especially scary for me to let go of the comfort of having had such a positive first experience, and the fear of the unknown out there was huge for me.

Even though I wanted to run from the intense feelings, I let myself cry and grieve the loss of this person who was such a major part of my daily life.

I didn't hold anything in, and I think that's what allowed me to be cleansed of the pain. Nothing was trapped inside, so I could be clear and open to eventually make room for someone new.

It's so hard when they were the one you shared your pain with and now they're the cause of it.

~~It's so hard when~~

Feeling the pain doesn't necessarily mean you have to just sit in a dark room and cry (though for some of us, that might be the answer). Here's Ava's story about how she channeled her pain into creativity to help her feel and process it.

AVA'S STORY:

MEDIUM

"He was my everything"

I just went through a breakup where I got my heart torn to pieces. We dated for ten months - it was the longest I'd ever been with someone. We knew every single thing about each other. It felt like we were married, we were that close.

Suddenly, one day, out of the blue, he stopped talking to me. He plays varsity soccer and went to a pre-season weekend away, and one of his stupid friends told him I had one of my friends keep an eye on him. Meanwhile, that was a total rumor, but he believed it anyway and got really pissed at me. I asked him why he was being so weird and he just went psycho on me.

He was my best friend, my confidante, and now if I talked to him at school he would tell me to shut up. It was so traumatizing, because it was like, where did you go?! I got sent home from school because I was so sick over this whole thing. To this day, I have no idea what happened.

I just feel so lost. The only way I'm coping is by playing guitar and writing songs. I've just been pouring all my feelings into my music, and that makes me feel more grounded. Some of the stuff I'm writing is so raw... this pain I'm going through is a nightmare but at the very least it's helping me go deeper with my music. Right now, that's what's getting me through this.

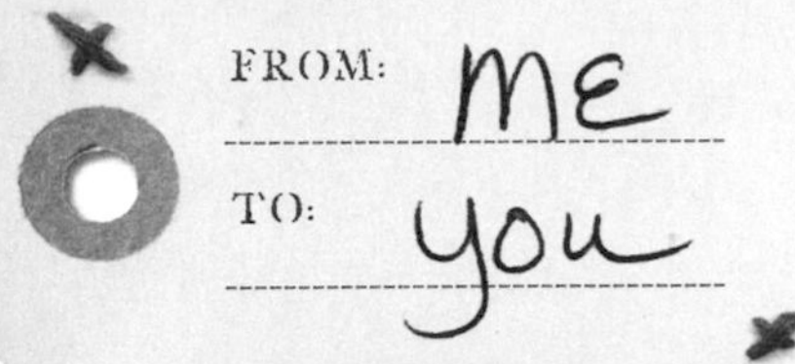

WE DON'T ALWAYS GET THE ANSWERS WE NEED

In instances like Ava's, it's so normal to think, "What did I do?" Of course you'd be dissecting every conversation looking for clues. But if someone turns on you and abandons you like this, ninety-nine percent of the time it has nothing to do with you. They might be going through private things we might never know, even if we feel we know them so well.

I think eighteen-year-old Zareen had a beautiful take on getting the closure you're craving: "Realizing it's okay to be unhappy about something is a part of growing up. Not everything always gets all wrapped up in a neat bow. Sometimes you just have to live with the fact that something happened that isn't fair, and that you don't have the answers. It's really hard, and it's really painful, but you have to grieve, feel sorry for yourself for a while, and at a certain point let it go and realize that if you keep dwelling on it, you're giving that person your energy and power." XOE

Create New Beginnings

You've been through a lot. Once the pain starts to subside (and it will, I promise), it's time to create a new reality that you love. This is the moment to start to make some positive and healthy changes within yourself and your life, and look for ways to emerge stronger from what you've been through. When we put the focus back on our own growth, the way the girls you're about to hear from did, we almost can't help but start to feel better.

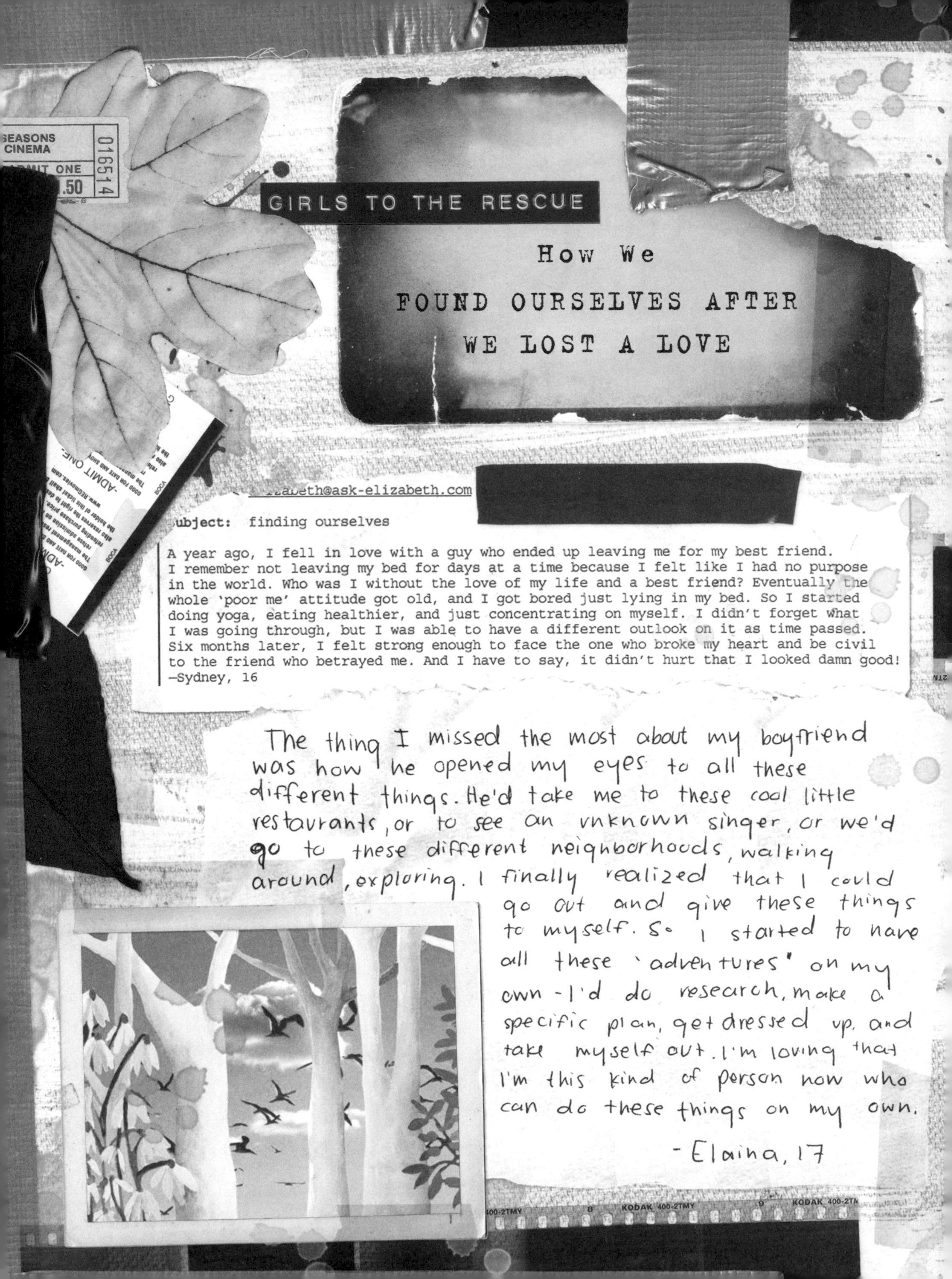

How We FOUND OURSELVES AFTER WE LOST A LOVE

elizabeth@ask-elizabeth.com

Subject: finding ourselves

A year ago, I fell in love with a guy who ended up leaving me for my best friend. I remember not leaving my bed for days at a time because I felt like I had no purpose in the world. Who was I without the love of my life and a best friend? Eventually the whole 'poor me' attitude got old, and I got bored just lying in my bed. So I started doing yoga, eating healthier, and just concentrating on myself. I didn't forget what I was going through, but I was able to have a different outlook on it as time passed. Six months later, I felt strong enough to face the one who broke my heart and be civil to the friend who betrayed me. And I have to say, it didn't hurt that I looked damn good!
—Sydney, 16

The thing I missed the most about my boyfriend was how he opened my eyes to all these different things. He'd take me to these cool little restaurants, or to see an unknown singer, or we'd go to these different neighborhoods, walking around, exploring. I finally realized that I could go out and give these things to myself. So I started to have all these 'adventures' on my own - I'd do research, make a specific plan, get dressed up, and take myself out. I'm loving that I'm this kind of person now who can do these things on my own.

- Elaina, 17

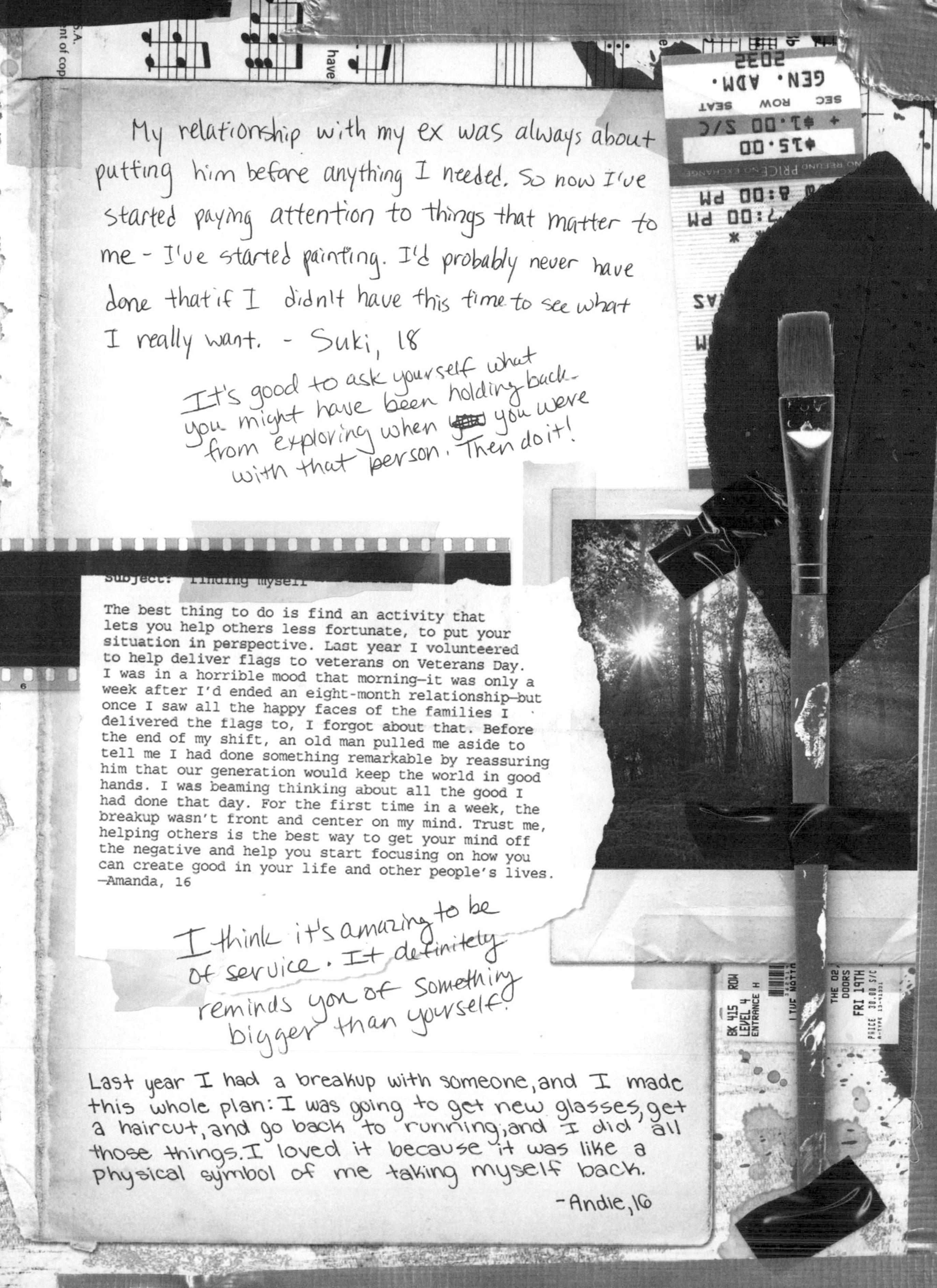

My relationship with my ex was always about putting him before anything I needed. So now I've started paying attention to things that matter to me - I've started painting. I'd probably never have done that if I didn't have this time to see what I really want. - Suki, 18

It's good to ask yourself what you might have been holding back from exploring when you were with that person. Then do it!

Subject: Finding Myself

The best thing to do is find an activity that lets you help others less fortunate, to put your situation in perspective. Last year I volunteered to help deliver flags to veterans on Veterans Day. I was in a horrible mood that morning—it was only a week after I'd ended an eight-month relationship—but once I saw all the happy faces of the families I delivered the flags to, I forgot about that. Before the end of my shift, an old man pulled me aside to tell me I had done something remarkable by reassuring him that our generation would keep the world in good hands. I was beaming thinking about all the good I had done that day. For the first time in a week, the breakup wasn't front and center on my mind. Trust me, helping others is the best way to get your mind off the negative and help you start focusing on how you can create good in your life and other people's lives.
—Amanda, 16

I think it's amazing to be of service. It definitely reminds you of something bigger than yourself.

Last year I had a breakup with someone, and I made this whole plan: I was going to get new glasses, get a haircut, and go back to running, and I did all those things. I loved it because it was like a physical symbol of me taking myself back.

-Andie, 16

An added bonus of working on ourselves to make ourselves better and stronger is that next time around, we can be part of a healthier relationship. I love how sixteen-year-old Katie described this:

There's a fine line between leaning on someone you love and being overly dependent.

A friend of mine once drew an analogy between a working relationship and two sticks. In the unhealthy relationship, one or both of the sticks was leaning on the other for support. In the healthy relationship, the sticks were depicted standing side by side, each supporting themselves.

HEALING TOOL #4

Set Yourself Free

Technically, it's called "acceptance".

How do we finally move on? Letting go is the final piece in any grief process, and there are (thankfully!) concrete actions you can take to exit victim mode and finally start to move forward.

- **Stop trying to win him back.** Believe me, I know it can take a long time to admit to ourselves that something is really over. You might go through a lot of rounds of make-ups and breakups, and hanging out in that painful place of not knowing where you stand. But when we know in our hearts that it's done, it's time to finally stop trying to win him back or make him feel sorry he lost you. That just keeps you hooked in, and we're looking to set you free, girlfriend!

- **No more spying on him.** C'mon, admit it: you're still spying on your ex, aren't you? I know it's so tempting to keep checking in on what he's doing, but ask yourself how you feel every time you get a piece of information or see a picture of him online living his life without you. Not so great, right? I know it's hard, but it's time to step away from the info flow. Sixteen-year-old Tara said, "At the time

No judgment... we've all done that!

you're so consumed by those feelings that you could be on fire and it wouldn't matter. That's when I think you need to listen hard to your good friends. If they're telling you to stop, *STOP!*"

Take some time away from him. If you can easily maintain a platonic friendship right away, that's great and rare, but for a lot of us that isn't possible. So you might need to put some space between you and your ex. I know you might crave keeping that connection alive, but deep down you know if the "friendship" is doing you more harm than good. If you secretly think that staying close to him will make him change his mind, if you're thinking about him now as a "friend" as much as you thought about him when you were together, if your mood is determined by whether you guys talk that day—those are all signs that maybe this friendship isn't the best thing for you right now. We can't let go and hold on at the same time, know what I mean?

Forgive him. This is a hard one, especially if he betrayed you. But for your own sake, you need to release the person with love in your heart. I know you might feel stuck on the details or injustice of what happened, but we're looking for you to let go of your anger for the sake of your future happiness. It's important to remember that just because one person did something to you doesn't mean that others will, too. A new person is exactly that—new. No two people are the same, so we need to release the past anger to be able to open our hearts and trust again. For more on forgiveness, take a look at the section titled "What do you do when a friendship you've had for a really long time falls apart?"

Release any regret. It's so common for us in the midst of heartbreak to feel like the relationship was a huge mistake or that it was a waste of our time and energy. But I promise you, holding on to regret gives you absolutely nothing. If anything, it drains you and blocks you from any of the good things coming your way right now. How can we regret anything that made us happy once and contributed to our lives in a way that helped us grow? As much as you can, try to focus on the gratitude for the good moments you shared. Those are your memories to keep, and whatever you learned from this person is yours now to apply and carry into your own life.

You've heard me say that every challenge we go through is a gift, and breakups are no exception. You'll never be the same . . . but why would you want to be? Though they can be messy and painful, you always take something out of them that makes you better in some way. Even the pain you feel now during the breakup process is deepening your wisdom and capacity to feel. While your heart might be breaking, it's also expanding in ways you can't imagine yet. Think about it—how else could you know how deep your emotions could go unless you went through this?

Look Forward, Not Back

When you're finally out of the brutal-pain part and you start moving on, you'll probably feel a rush and a burst of new hope. It can feel like the world is all about new beginnings for you—and it is.

Now's the perfect time to get clear on what you truly want and deserve in your future relationships. So even though this might not sound romantic, get out your journal and make a list of your ex's qualities that you loved. For example, if you loved that your ex treated you with respect or you loved the deep talks you two shared, write those things down.

Or even write somewhere in this book!

Then start a second list where you'll write the things that maybe you didn't have in that relationship but that you now know are important to you in your future relationships. Let's say romance is important to you and he was anything but romantic—or maybe he was kind of serious all the time and you know now that a sense of humor is a must for you. Don't judge what you want. . . . Dream big.

I know it's hard to think of anyone else right now, but you can thank me later when Mr. Right comes along!

Remember, no rush

You're probably thinking, *Elizabeth, why am I doing this?* Here's why: because on paper, you will see clearly what you need, desire, and deserve. While the details are still fresh in your mind, you get to take an inventory of your relationship to know what worked, what didn't, and why. This way, when you're ready, you can actively choose what you want the next time. I promise, you're far more likely to meet the guy of your dreams if you have a clear picture of what that relationship actually looks like. That's called "manifesting."

Always know that no matter how much your heart has been broken, your ability to love is yours—no one can ever give that to you or take that from you; it's within you. I'm so excited for you to meet the next guy who gets the lucky gift of your love—now from your expanded and even more powerful heart.

BFFs,
BULLIES,
and
To a great friend

3

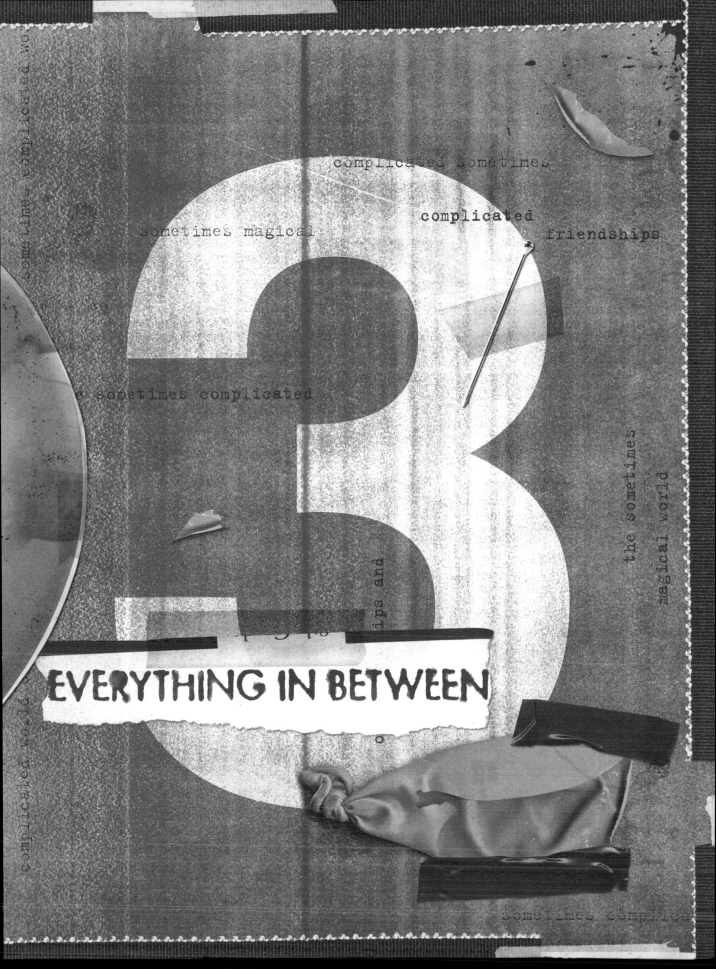

EVERYTHING IN BETWEEN

THE (sometimes) COMPLICATED AND (sometimes) MAGICAL WORLD OF FRIENDSHIPS

* *

Where would any of us be without our incredible friends?

I mean, who else can you laugh, cry, be silly, and share your secrets with—not to mention turn to when you need a little love and support. Yes, of course, some of us have that with our families...but the special thing about friends is that they're the family we actually get to choose.

As beautiful and precious as our friendships can be, they still have their tough moments. In this chapter, we're going to dig beneath the surface and talk about some friendship issues that can be challenging or confusing. Like when a friend does something that hurts our feelings...the torture of having to "confront" her, right? It's never easy, but here you'll find a ton of tools and tips that can empower you to speak up to a friend when you need to.

We'll also talk about one of the hardest things we have to deal with: when a friendship falls apart. It's sad and painful and scary, and so many of us have been through it, so we're here to help you if you're dealing with that kind of loss.

We'll also break down another tough topic here: mean girls. You know who I'm talking about—the nasty girls who gang up on someone, suddenly decide to exclude her, or worse, are out to ruin her life. It's a sad reality that those girls are out there, but if any of you find yourself the target, I can promise that there's help for you in here. No more suffering in silence, and no more being anyone's victim.

Whether we're dealing with a friend or a frenemy, every relationship we have makes us deeper, stronger, and smarter. → Yes, even the mean girls. Some bring us joy and love and laughter, and others challenge us to find out what we're really made of. So before you jump into this chapter, let's just all say a silent thank-you to every person who gets us a little bit closer to who we truly are.

Date

If a friend hurts your feelings, how do you confront her without making her mad??

Here's the truth: if you have to confront a friend about something she's done that upset you, the reality is that she *might* get mad! We can't control someone else's reactions. What we can control, though, is how we communicate our truth, our willingness to listen, and how we respond in return. All it takes is one calm person in the mix to prevent a potentially touchy conversation from exploding into World War III.

Hopefully with respect and love.

I know the word "confront" has such a negative and dramatic vibe to it, but honestly, it doesn't always have to mean a big argument. So maybe let's replace that word in our minds with something new. How about "speaking your truth"? To me, that feels better because what we're really talking about here is taking care of yourself by communicating what's in your heart.

If we do it right, we can fully skip the drama and get right to the heart-to-heart stuff

So many of us stress out and waste tons of time and energy trying to avoid conflict. I don't know anyone who likes making waves. But just think how much better and stronger your bonds of friendship would be—not to mention your self-confidence—if you channeled all that energy into learning to speak your truth. No more pretending you're cool with a situation that's secretly hurting you . . . no more being afraid to say what's on your mind. How freeing would that be?

And not just to your friends... with everyone in your life!

"Am I Making Too Much of This?"

It can be tricky to know when you should speak up about something, and when it's better to just let it go and resolve the feelings within yourself. I get that we don't want to make more out of a situation than it is. . . . But then again, we don't want to allow ourselves to be taken advantage of or hurt, either. So how do we know when we're making too much out of something and when we need to speak up?

For me, it comes down to three questions I ask myself.

* *Is it a pattern that keeps showing up or a onetime minor thing in the bigger picture of our friendship?*
* *Is this going to consistently bug me if I don't say something, or am I truly okay letting go of this?*
* *Does it feel intentional, or do I think she didn't even realize it?*

Friends might hurt our feelings now and then without meaning to; we're all human. If it's something that was an oversight or is minor in the bigger picture of our friendship, I let it go and trust that my friends love me and know that I love them. Like one time when I was at a party and one of my closest girlfriends grabbed two of her other friends to go into a photo booth to take a strip of silly pictures. I was standing nearby, and in the moment it stung a little that she didn't ask me to join. But I quickly reminded myself that she would never intentionally hurt me and probably was just caught up in the fun of the moment. So I didn't feel like I needed to bring it up to her. On the other hand, if that was something that was happening with us a lot (my feeling left out), or if it was something that was really hurtful that I wasn't okay with letting go of (like if I knew she'd seen me standing there and purposely didn't ask me to hop in with them), then I would know I had to say something.

No one likes feeling left out.

See the difference?

Here's sixteen-year-old Jordan's story about knowing when it becomes necessary to speak up. . . .

JORDAN'S STORY: "It Kept Happening"

I had a group of friends who I was very close to, but this year I went to a different school and there were a lot of times when they didn't include me in their plans. I would call and ask what they were doing, and it was always "We're not sure yet," or something like that, and then I wouldn't hear back from them. In the beginning I told myself not to take it personally, but it was really frustrating and upsetting for me because I felt not wanted.

I hate getting into fights with friends, and I was worried that they would say I was just being paranoid, so instead I started being passive-aggressive... like saying kind of sarcastically, "So, did you guys have a good time on Saturday?" I didn't like how I was acting, and I definitely didn't like how I was feeling.

Eventually, it was bothering me enough that I knew I had to say something. I called one of them who I have a really good relationship with and said, "I have to tell you something that's been really bothering me, because your friendship is important to me and I want to work this out. Every time I call I feel like you guys are avoiding me. Can you tell me what's going on?" She explained that sometimes the plans were just spontaneous, and they weren't meaning to leave me out. Because I wasn't right there at school to be automatically included, she said they'd be sure to call or text me from then on to see if I wanted to come. I'm so happy I spoke up, because they really are good friends and they did start to make efforts to include me more.

The next time you're wondering whether a situation warrants a confrontation, try asking yourself those three questions I mentioned (Is it a pattern? Will it keep bugging me if I don't speak up? Was it intentional?), and you'll know the answer pretty quickly.

Why Bother Speaking Up?

"I don't want to start a whole big thing."
"It's just easier to forget about it."
"I don't want to lose her as a friend, and I'm scared I will if I say something."

Have you ever said something like this to yourself when you're angry or upset with a friend, even though you know you should talk to her about it? Be honest!

I know it might seem easier to downplay your feelings, but there are really good reasons you should—actually, why you need to—express them to your friend.

REASON TO SPEAK UP #1

Real Friendships Are Based on Truth

If you tell someone something from your heart, and they are really your friend, they'll know you're being sincere and respond the same way, even if they don't agree with you. My goal is to be honest with my friends in a noble and loving way. ~ Lisette, 16

Sure, it's easy to have fun with people, and the temptation might be to act like everything is great even if it's not, but is that really what you want in your relationships? One of the signs of a true friendship is that you can both feel safe enough to share your private feelings and secrets—even the messy, uncomfortable ones. A friendship that's solid like this can withstand a little friction in the name of being honest with each other.

It's so normal to worry that bringing up problems or issues might break apart our friendships, but ironically, it's the clumsy, confrontational moments that actually can end up bringing us closer together. Think about it: have you ever been through something tough with a friend—maybe a big fight or even a heart-to-heart discussion about something that wasn't going right between you—that you worked through? Didn't you feel so much closer to her after you guys cleared the air?

I'm not saying to intentionally create conflict—ha!

ELIZABETH BERKLEY

Even the friends who know us best might not have a clue that something is bothering us until we tell them. I've told you about how close my BFF Seane and I are. Seane travels the world teaching yoga and doing incredible activism work, and I have my acting projects, creative pursuits, and cross-country travels giving Ask Elizabeth workshops. Because of our hectic schedules, we don't get to spend a lot of time together, but our love for each other and our faith in our friendship keeps us bonded.

There was a point, though, when I started to really miss sharing the girly, day-to-day stuff, like, "OMG, you'll never guess who I saw today.... I read the funniest thing and thought of you.... You have to see this new dress I just got...." We were always there for each other in a crisis, but somehow the fun little details were getting lost in the shuffle.

I was afraid to mention that I'd been feeling like I was the one doing all the calling and e-mailing, and that I wanted her to reach out a little bit more, because I didn't want it to feel like pressure. At the same time, this had been on my mind for a while, so I felt like it was important to bring it up.

<And who wants to feel like an obligation? Ew!

The next time we were both in Los Angeles at the same time, we met for lunch. I'll admit it: I was nervous!
I was also hesitant to say something, since we have such limited time together in person and I wanted our lunch to be fun. But I decided that since the foundation of our closeness is being real with each other, I owed it to us to say something. I told her that I was so proud of all the incredible things she was doing in the world but that I missed her and sharing our everyday things. I explained that I wasn't asking for daily check-ins or anything like that but that hearing from her more often would be great.

Seane & me ♥

She seemed surprised at first but then quickly said that she didn't realize I felt that way. Just being able to tell her what I had been holding in made me feel so much closer to her. After that, I'd get sweet texts here and there from her, like, "Hi, just landed in London, thinking about you!" A few weeks later, she actually thanked me because she said she'd realized how much she was missing those small-but-meaningful exchanges, too. --XOE

Seane's loving response to what I said was a relief. But as we know, a friend might get angry, upset, or defensive when she hears what you have to say, and it's important to be open to her reaction. Once you've said your piece, you have to let her speak her mind. If hearing her side makes you anxious, or if you're the one confronted, my advice is to just breathe through your instinct to immediately attack and defend your position, and remember that the goal is to get the friendship to a better place—it's not about having to be "right."

Not fun, but let's keep it real!

REASON TO SPEAK UP #2

Ignoring Something Doesn't Make It Go Away

Doesn't it suck that you're hurt but you're so worried about making her upset that you just ignore what she said? It doesn't help, though, because ultimately it'll end up coming out some other way. –Jerri, 15

The thing about anger or hurt feelings is that it has to go *somewhere.* Unless you express it to the person, the emotion just stays bottled up and you end up living with this underlying tension and weirdness. You might be keeping your friend happy, but you know who gets hurt here: you.

We're so quick to betray ourselves and our feelings in the name of being nice and keeping the peace, but every time we do that we harm ourselves a little bit. Any time we feel an internal struggle, it's because we're going against what we know in our bones is right for us. Yeah, it could seem easier to stay quiet than to stay true to yourself, but at what cost?

At workshops all across the country, I've asked you guys to tell me how you feel when you don't stay true to yourselves and speak up. . . .

• Angry • Like crap • Alone • Guilty • Scared of getting in trouble • Not like the true me • Awkward, out of place, uncomfortable • Annoyed with myself • Sick • Ashamed • Disgusted with myself • Like crying

Quite a list of reasons to speak up, isn't it? In moments when you're questioning whether to speak your truth to a friend—or anyone else, for that matter—I think it's important to ask yourself, *How will I feel if I don't speak up?*

Those feelings, like we said, can't just get wished away, and they'll end up surfacing sooner or later. As sixteen-year-old Chloe said, "If you don't say something about what's raging inside of you, it will blow up. And then it's usually much uglier than it would have been if you'd just spoken from your heart in the first place."

Which is exactly what happened to fifteen-year-old Suzanne . . .

SUZANNE'S STORY: "I tried to let it slide" 

When I was in middle school, I had this best friend. We both liked the same guy, and he kind of liked me, but I told her that if it was going to make her upset I wouldn't go for it. But she said, "No, no, go ahead," and so I did. I assumed she meant what she said.

A few weeks later I started hearing all these crazy random rumors about me, like I was letting him sneak into my house at night, and I found out that they were coming from her. I was blown away. At first I said, "Okay, I'll let it slide; she's just upset that I'm going out with him, and I have to understand." I started hearing more and more, and I kept telling myself I should ignore it, even though I was really pissed off.

And then I heard that she told people that I was pregnant, and that's when something in my brain just clicked and I went nuts on her. Everyone was shocked because I'm a passive person. I just had all this anger built up in me, and I totally let loose on her.

It took a lot of talks and texts and crying, but we did eventually patch things up. I learned a lot from that experience. Now when someone does something to me, I'll call them out on it right away. I'll just say, "Hey, can you tell me what the problem is so we can work it out?" I'm honest with people and let them know exactly how I feel, so there's no miscommunication and things don't build up to the point of no return.

REASON TO SPEAK UP #3

Speaking Your Truth Builds Your Inner Strength

A step at a time... That's the only way to get over the fear of sticking up for yourself. And once you start to do it, you see that it's almost never as horrible as you think it's going to be

— Jessie, 18

This probably won't be a surprise to you, but fear is the biggest reason we hold back from speaking our truth. Fear of creating drama . . . of being thought of as a bitch . . . of losing the friendship (and then losing all your other friends, too) . . . It's a long list of fears you've all talked about. I think fifteen-year-old Yvonne pretty much nailed what I've heard a lot of other girls confess to feeling: "I hate being in fights and being in drama. I just feel sick whenever someone gets mad at me. . . . I get scared of everything: their tone, that they'll tell me they don't want to be friends with me anymore, that I won't be able to defend myself. . . ."

But our fears don't have to get the best of us; we actually can overcome them by shrinking them down to size. Whenever I feel nervous about communicating a hard truth to someone, I ask myself, *What's my worst fear about what could happen?* Naming the fear helps to defuse it and take away its power to paralyze me.

Let's say that my fear is that I'll lose my friend if I tell her that she did something that hurt me. I can then ask myself, *Is that fear realistic?* Based on our history as friends, if it isn't, then I know I'm letting my imagination create all kinds of negative scenarios that have nothing to do with reality. If I think that losing

Amazing how creative our imaginations can be when we're imagining the worst her actually is a possibility, then I take it to the next step, which is to ask myself, *Well, okay, what if that did happen?* I keep asking myself the question *And then what?* over and over, until I play out the scenario in my head all the way to the point where I know I'd ultimately be okay. It might go something like this:

I'd be really sad . . . and lonely . . . I'd miss her.

And then what?

I would know the friendship wasn't as strong as I thought it was, because being honest and open with my friends should be okay.

And then what?

I'd turn to my other good friends for support. I'd be okay, because I would know in my heart that I did everything I could, even if the friendship didn't work out the way I wanted it to.

See what I mean? In other words, by letting myself imagine the absolute worst-case scenario and seeing that I would still survive even if it did happen, the fear doesn't have any power over me anymore. Now, of course, most of the time our worst fear never turns into reality. But this is a great tool to use whenever you have a big fear of any kind staring you in the face. It's amazing how empowered you'll feel when you start to defuse your fears like this.

Think of speaking up for yourself like working out: each time you do it, you get a little bit stronger, a little bit better at it.

Tips on Speaking Up

Okay, so now you know when and why it's important to speak up if your feelings have been hurt. . . . Now you ready for the "how" part?

Thoughts and Advice for How to Handle

FRIENDSHIP FRICTION

I learned this thing where you say 'I am feeling this way,' or 'I felt hurt when....' instead of saying 'you.' 'you did this' or 'you made me feel...' It's such a great tool, because the person doesn't get defensive. It keeps the responsibility on you and lets them know you aren't attacking them but instead are trying to work things out. -Amanda, 16

This is key to communicating without creating drama.

BE ST FRI ENDS

Clas

Whatever you do, don't do it over e-mail or text. Trust me, I made that mistake with my guy BFF. Talk to me face-to-face, or even on the phone, so you can avoid ~~my~~ any misunderstandings —Kara, 16

To: < elizabeth@ask-elizabeth.com >

Subject: Friendship Friction

When I confront people, I can sometimes be too aggressive, so I have to really work on doing it in a compassionate way. I've learned that if you have a strong personality you can't just use that with everyone...especially not with people who are more sensitive. Be gentle if you're dealing with a friend who needs that. It doesn't mean don't bring it up; it just means do it with kindness. —Tucker, 18

It's so important to approach your friend in a way that she can hear you. —E

I think that if you have something you know you need to talk to a friend about, it's good to communicate up front that you're bringing it up because you care about the friendship—then you can get your point across and it won't turn into a big fight. —Erica, 15

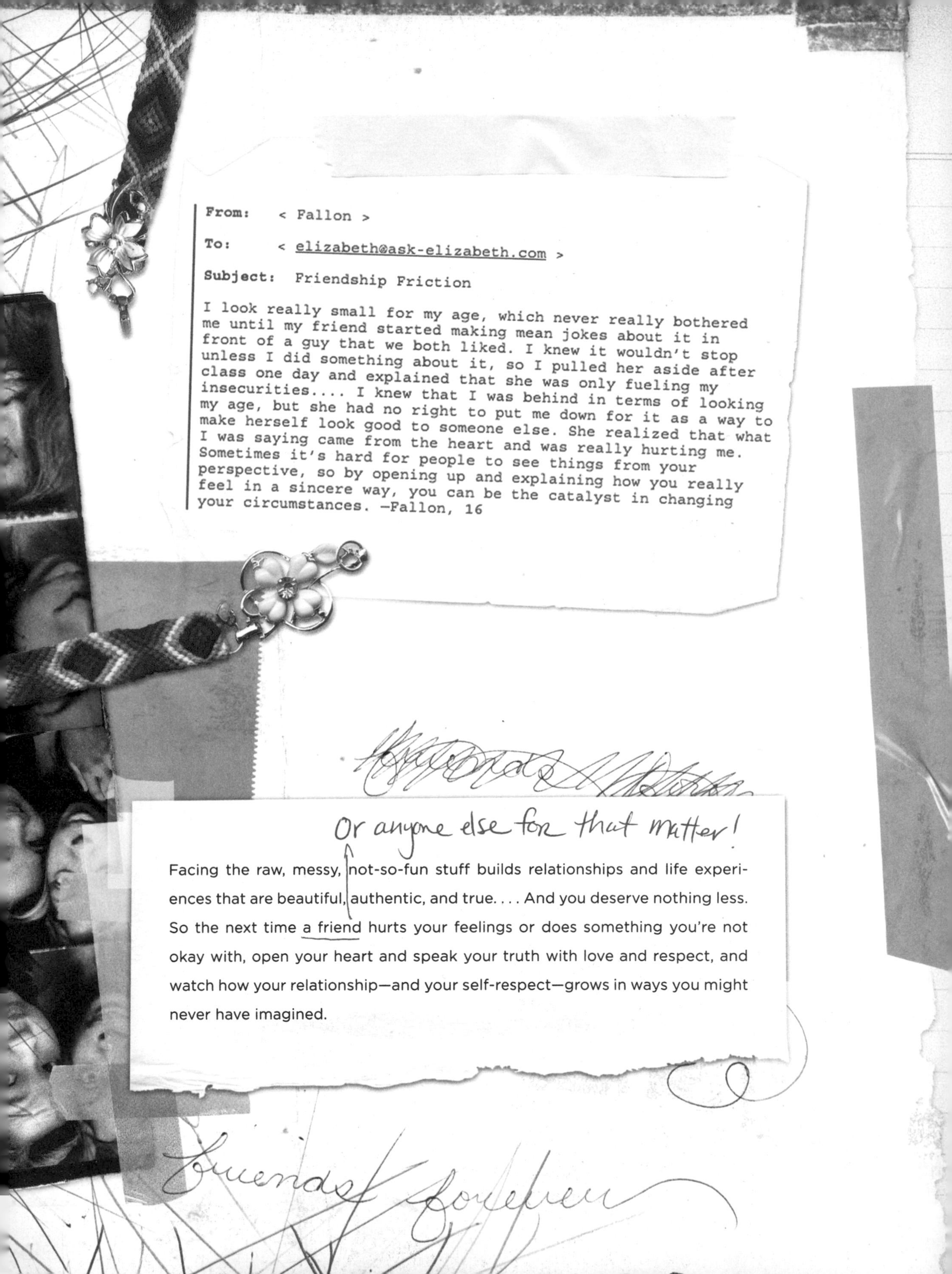

From: < Fallon >

To: < elizabeth@ask-elizabeth.com >

Subject: Friendship Friction

I look really small for my age, which never really bothered me until my friend started making mean jokes about it in front of a guy that we both liked. I knew it wouldn't stop unless I did something about it, so I pulled her aside after class one day and explained that she was only fueling my insecurities.... I knew that I was behind in terms of looking my age, but she had no right to put me down for it as a way to make herself look good to someone else. She realized that what I was saying came from the heart and was really hurting me. Sometimes it's hard for people to see things from your perspective, so by opening up and explaining how you really feel in a sincere way, you can be the catalyst in changing your circumstances. —Fallon, 16

Or anyone else for that matter!

Facing the raw, messy, not-so-fun stuff builds relationships and life experiences that are beautiful, authentic, and true. . . . And you deserve nothing less. So the next time a friend hurts your feelings or does something you're not okay with, open your heart and speak your truth with love and respect, and watch how your relationship—and your self-respect—grows in ways you might never have imagined.

friends forever

A group of girls is making my life completely MISERABLE and I don't know what to do...

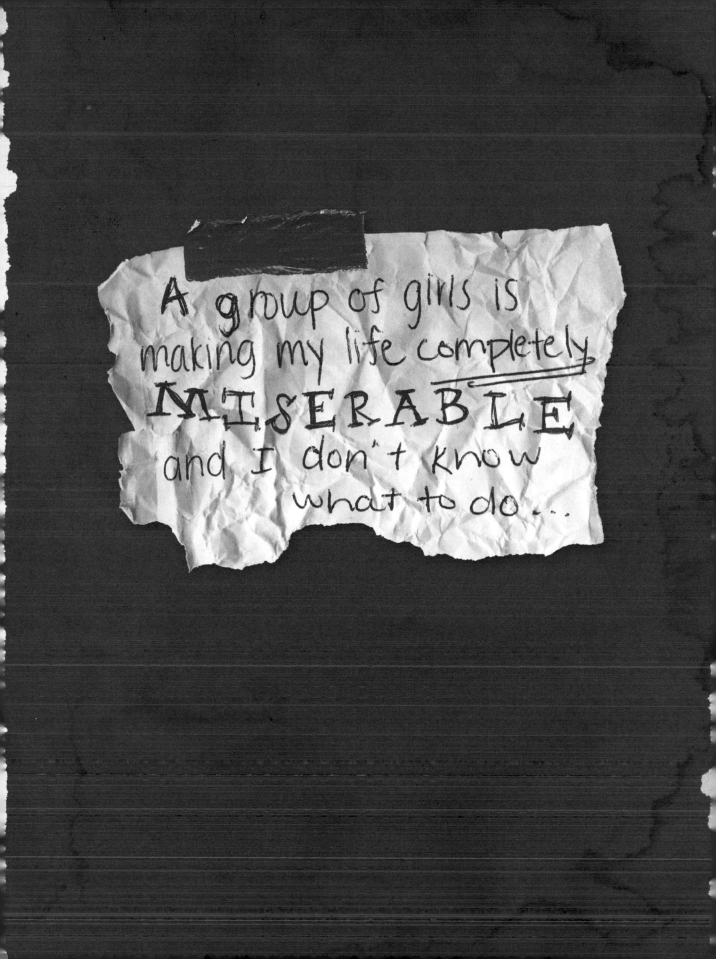

It's so crazy—as supportive and amazing as girls can be to each other, they can also be total nightmares. But you don't need me to tell you that, right? You're living it.

Trust me, I know that finding yourself the target of nasty people who are out to take you down can be a scary and deeply lonely experience. I've been there. The situation I want to share with you wasn't in high school, actually—it was a few years later. But honestly, it doesn't matter whether it happens in school hallways, online, or in the press—any time you feel ganged up on or powerless, it's bullying. Here's what happened.

ELIZABETH BERKLEY

Or so I thought! ☹

Early in my acting career, I landed the movie role of my dreams. I had gone up against thousands of girls to land this role, including some of the biggest names in Hollywood. I'd worked my entire life to get to this moment and thought that all my dreams were finally about to come true.

Let's just say that the movie wasn't a success. From the moment it opened, my life was a blur of some of the nastiest comments ever written about a film, or an actress in it. It wasn't the bad reviews of the film that got to me; it was that the attacks in the press were personal--so vicious that loved ones tried to hide them from me. I actually had one journalist sit across from me during an interview, smiling and casually sipping iced tea, asking, "How does it feel to be a failure?" The attacks just kept coming. People seemed to get off on joining in, like, "Let's jump in, she's an easy target!"

I'm not kidding!

Not one person who was involved with the movie came to my defense--I was out there alone with my self-esteem in shreds. By the time the dust settled, I was a pariah. I had my head handed to me on a national level, and my heart wanted to know why. --XOE

I'll get to the rest of this story in a bit, but I wanted to share that part with you right up front so you know that when I say I get it, you know I *really* get it. For you guys right now, mean girls are the ones who are trying to take you down and make you feel utterly worthless; for me, it was the industry I work in (which, trust me, is a lot more like high school than you think!). Either way, being the punching bag . . . well, let's be real: it sucks.

This was such a defining experience in my life because it taught me how to save my self-esteem and rise above that kind of ugliness. It's one of the biggest reasons why I'm here for you. We're going to get you through this and help you get stronger within yourself so their brutal behavior, nasty comments, texts, IMs, whatever, can't get to you anymore. No way are we going to let their cruelty take you down.

I'm not the only one who understands the feelings you're going through. I swear, I don't think I've been to a single school anywhere in the country where this isn't happening to at least one girl. . . .

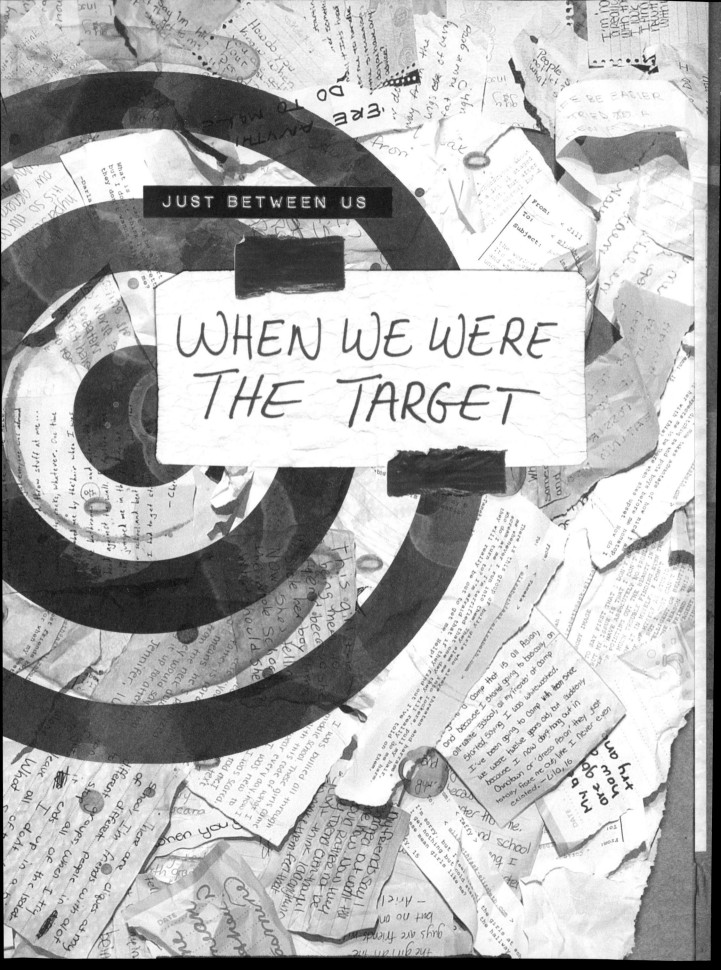

JUST BETWEEN US

WHEN WE WERE THE TARGET

I go to a camp that is all Asian, and because I started going to basically an all-white school, all my 'friends' at camp started saying I was whitewashed. I've been going to camp with them since we were twelve years old, but suddenly because I now don't hang out in Chinatown or 'dress Asian' they just totally froze me out, like I never even existed. —Lila, 16

I was bullied all through middle school. These girls came up with this code of what I had to wear every day, how I wore my hair. I was new to the school, and I was scared, so I did what they told me. I would get these horrible text messages, like 'You're retarded,' 'You smell like cheese,' 'You're a bitch.' My father is paraplegic, which means he's paralyzed from the neck down, and they would say I was making it up for attention.

- Jennifer, 16

This girl at school suddenly got fixated on me and decided to make my life HELL. She was the kind of girl everyone was ~~afraid~~ scared of. She'd throw stuff at me . . . cigarette butts, rocks, whatever. One time she grabbed me by the hair when I was at the bathroom and slammed my head against the wall. Another time she jumped me in the parking lot after school and beat me up so badly that I had to get stitches in my lip.

—Cheryl, 15

To: < elizabeth@ask-elizabeth.com >

A few months ago this group of girls started posting things online about me, like 'You whore, you bitch,' just because I started dating a guy that one of them used to go out with. They actually created a 'We Hate Lisa' website that was full of mean videos that said things like 'We hope you die.' The worst thing is that I know that some of them are just doing it because they're bored.
—Lisa, 17

Why Are Some Girls So Mean?

Yeah, don't we all want the answer to that?

I know that right now, if it's happening to you, the last thing you care about is what makes the girls who are torturing you the way they are. But I think it helps to understand where a lot of it is coming from, because when you see that it rarely has anything to do with *you* and everything to do with *them,* it can help make it feel less personal for you.

~~Even tho~~ Even though it feels like it.

Here's what it comes down to: girls are mean for one basic reason, and that's insecurity. Anytime anyone is taking shots at you—whether with words or fists—it's almost always in an attempt to make herself feel better. Some try to get power by being the queen bee because they're afraid of losing their "status." Others might be jealous of you, so they lash out at you to try to make you shine a little less.

Not that this lets them off the hook!

The key words here are "try to"

Some have so much anger and hurt inside that they need to spew onto someone, and you're just the unlucky random target.

Here's firsthand proof from seventeen-year-old Theresa.

THERESA'S STORY: "I had to let out all the pain inside me"

For my whole life, I had the best mom you could ever want. She would do everything with me, and I loved her so much. Then when my little sister was born she became bi-polar, and the mom I loved so much was just completely gone. I was just so angry at the whole world, like why did this have to happen? I just had all this anger inside me, and I guess whenever I would see a girl who seemed vulnerable it would remind me of how vulnerable I was actually feeling... I would just flip out and start fighting her. It wasn't about the other person there was just so much that was going on within me that my outlet was beating up on them. At a certain point I had to ask myself why I was doing this. I started realizing I was hurting these girls because I was in so much pain that I had to let it out. I had all these issues at home, and I think I was craving the attention. It came to a point where I would look at a girl's bloody face when the fight was done and I would ask myself who deserves that? I realized that hurting her wouldn't help me hurt any less. I was just passing the hate around. I needed to get the pain out another way— through healing what was going on within myself.

Although the stupid comments and horrible behavior bullies are sending your way can feel like poison darts to your soul (or, if it's physical abuse, humiliating and painful), I really want you to get that you didn't ask for it. It's not your fault, and no matter what, you definitely don't deserve it.

There are always going to be haters out there in the world, and they're going to do what they do. We can't control that. What we can control, though, is what we do in the face of their brutality. Do we let it take us down and dictate how we feel about ourselves? Or can we take back our power and refuse to allow ourselves to be the victims? (Hint: it's the second one. . . . read on!)

ACTION STEPS: Triumph Over The Torment

When people are spewing all kinds of mean, nasty stuff at us, it's so normal to buy into what they are saying and allow it to beat us down. But I promise you, there are other options. No more letting what they say or do dictate your life and your belief in yourself . . . We're going to help you find your way through this. It's time to take action to get those haters out of your life—and your head.

There isn't a one-answer-fits-all solution for dealing with mean girls; you'll need to use your instincts to know which of the action steps here are right for your specific situation. But I'm guessing that at least one of these (if not more) will resonate as a way for you to finally get some peace.

ACTION STEP # 1

Confront the Mean Girl (if It Feels Safe)

This is probably the last thing you can imagine doing right now, right? I've heard from a lot of you that either you feel like it won't matter or you're worried it will just make the situation worse. There are ways (and reasons) to stand up to her (or them) that might actually help the situation.

I wanted to get as much help for you on this as possible, so I reached out to a few experts I know and respect, including author Rachel Simmons, who wrote an amazing book about girl relationships called *Odd Girl Out*. She works with girls all around the world, giving them strategies for dealing with bullies. Rachel made a great point about the power of standing up for yourself that I think is so worth taking in. . . .

ASK THE EXPERTS

"LEADERSHIP FOR LIFE" author

Rachel Simmons

on

Taking a Stand

There's much more that can be accomplished by speaking out than just solving the immediate problem. There are times when voicing your feelings is less about fixing something, and more about taking a stand, no matter what the outcome. You speak up to represent yourself, to make sure that you are listened to because you believe you're worthy of being heard. Speaking up is a way to value yourself in a moment when others are trying to cut you down. Whether or not you're successful is not the point. You are taking a stand: by yourself, for yourself.

Looove this!

I once met a woman in her early twenties who told me that when she was bullied in high school, her mother advised her to lie low. She did, but she felt like she was letting the others win through her silence. She felt that the others had not only hurt her but had taken away her voice, too. She told me she wished she could go back to high school and say something to the girls who hurt her.

Think about this: if you were writing your autobiography fifty years from now, and writing the chapter about the situation you're in right now, what would you want to remember? Would you want to write that you had remained quiet or spoken up? As Natasha Bedingfield sings, "Today is where your book begins / The rest is still unwritten." The pen is in your hands.

I couldn't agree more. I saw for myself how much power we can take back when we stand up for ourselves.

Back to the story I started to tell you earlier about the movie. From that time on, I've worked hard to choose to be in only quality projects and to continue to grow as an artist, and have appeared in many other successful movies, theater productions, and TV shows. Yet even though it was years later, there was a journalist who still chose to pick on me.

I was at an awards event one night, and a photographer took a picture of me talking to a famous playwright. The next day, a journalist wrote a straightforward story about the event...all except for his comment under that photo, which was: "The most surreal moment of the night was Elizabeth Berkley speaking to that playwright."

When I read that, my heart sank, because it completely invalidated everything I'd worked so hard to achieve.

It was as if he was saying that I didn't even deserve to be there, let alone talk to this person. If it was a review of a performance, okay.... I get that that's a critic's job. But this was personal--and he'd never even met me. I felt the same way I've heard so many of you talk about feeling when people cruelly exclude you or make you feel unwanted. It was like, "Enough is enough." So what, an actress was in a movie critics didn't like.... it happens. Move on, people!

The next day, I decided to call the journalist personally because I felt he abused his power at my expense. I calmly asked him if anyone had ever bullied him on the playground when he was a kid, and told him that was no different than him perpetuating the nastiness from my past, and that he should understand as a journalist that the people he writes about are human and what he says has an effect.

Remember the "how" of communicating is important

on," and was prepared to
Ms. Berkley was calling to register yet another grievance. She had read a reference I made to her presence at another awards ceremony, in a small picture-page item, and wanted to note her displeasure. My offense? I had identified her as the star of a movie

away the reference to an actress meeting a playwright. Nothing surreal there. To identify Ms. Berkley with her early-career debacle continually is to signal, however subtly, that it represents the totality of her achievement, and no, it's not fair. Who among us would like to be eternally judged by the clunkier moments in our own careers?

I recount this inconsequential history because

He just listened. There was no apology; I didn't get any satisfaction from his response. But after I hung up and took a deep breath (because believe me, that wasn't an easy call to make!) I felt frustrated, but I decided to focus on the satisfaction I felt from my own actions, knowing that I respected myself enough to stand up for myself.

matic debacle, she had

Cut to two years later. I was starring on Broadway, and little did I know that this journalist was in the audience one night. Two weeks later, to my surprise, an article appeared in The New York Times titled "The Redemption of Elizabeth Berkley." It was basically an open apology to me, in which he actually explained the call I had made to him, and said he'd wronged me in the past. Wow, right? I was pretty blown away. Clearly what I'd said had made an impact, and I was impressed by his willingness to admit this publicly, and the kindness and grace he showed me. --XOE

one of my biggest dreams!

While it was lovely that I got that rare closure, the true reward still came from making that phone call.

glas Kirkland/United Artis

were impressive,
from her
I had not
dentify her
utifully ign
ation, Ms.
as a spring
references
maging to her career. She would appreci-
f I refrained from making them.
ng up feeling guilty and chastened — emo-
ommonly supposed to be alien to critics.
s. Berkley had a point. Bad movies happen
actors all the time, but established actors
eputations to fall back on. When your rep-
-making movie is a celebrated dog, it can
ost impossible to fight free of the late-
lk show jokes and forge a path to respect-
For that matter, even big stars can have

kley handles the more baroque stretches of Mr. Rabe's dialogue with aplomb, and strikes a deeply poignant note in the play's second act, when Bobbie interrupts a drug-induced, nihilistic reverie from Mr. Hawke's character with a morsel of humanistic truth: Life may be a big, empty lie, but that's no excuse for being mean to your friends.

Ouch! That hits home: it's no excuse for being mean to actors, either. So don't ask me for the title of that movie. As I said, my lips are sealed.

I wanted to share this story with you so that you could see that you can stop being someone's victim *in your own mind,* just by taking a stand. If you decide to stand up to a bully in your world, know that you might not get the reaction from her (or him) that you want, but like Rachel said, that's not the point. You will know that you communicated that it's not okay to treat you badly, and your self-respect will be your reward.

Okay, so how can we get you that same kind of self-respecting satisfaction? I talked to another amazing expert named Rosalind Wiseman, who wrote the bestselling book *Queen Bees and Wannabees* (the book that the movie *Mean Girls* was based on). Rosalind told me she breaks down the process of confronting a mean girl into five steps, which I want to tell you about.

1 The first step Rosalind suggests is to write out the specific details of what happened, what the mean girl said to you or what she did to you, and what you want to have happen. This way, Rosalind says, "You're taking all those horrible feelings in your stomach and putting them down in words."

2 Next she suggests practicing having the conversation so you can get comfortable with the words you want to say (with someone you trust or in front of a mirror). I completely agree: rehearsing ahead of time is a great way to control nervousness.... How do you think performers get over stage fright?

3 When you're ready, Rosalind says it's best to talk to the mean girl somewhere where you feel safe (but not electronically, and not in front of all her friends!) and tell her straight-out what it is that she's doing that you don't like. For instance, "I know you started all these rumors about me."

4 After that, she says to follow it up by telling the mean girl what you want to have happen ("I want you to stop" is a straightforward but effective way to go).

5 End by suggesting how you two can coexist going forward. Rosalind's example was to say something like, "Look, you don't have to like me—just stop what you're doing and then we'll just stay away from each other."

eth Berkley mov

Rosalind added a last point that I think is important to remember: "Please know that almost all mean people, when confronted with their behavior, will blow you off. An eye roll or 'whatever' is probably as good as it's going to get—and that's fine. The goal isn't to get her to regret what she did, it's to get the behavior to stop, and the only way that will happen is if you communicate that you're not going to take it."

I want to say one last thing to you guys, and please hear me on this: I want you to consider confronting a bully only if it feels safe for you to do so. If you in any way feel like your well-being is being threatened, it's not the moment for working on standing up for yourself—it's the moment to be strong by reaching out for help. I'll talk about why and how to do that in action step #3, but for right now, I just want to make sure that you really check in with yourself before going to speak to a mean girl, to make sure that you're safe and protected. Promise me, okay?

ACTION STEP # 2

Take Away Their Power

Like we said before, girls are mean because it gives them a sense of power to take you down. They are measuring their worth according to how bad they can make you feel. It's sick but true. So you see, you have a lot more power here than you think! If you refuse to be taken down, they don't get the sense of satisfaction they are craving. Without the drama that makes it fun for them, they'll eventually get bored and move on.

When confronting a mean girl doesn't feel safe or you truly believe that it won't help the situation, another way to defuse an intense situation is to just *walk away.* This sounds simple, I know, but that doesn't mean it's easy . . . especially if it's a group of friends-turned-frenemies you're dealing with. Our instinct might be to hang on to the friendships even though we're being treated badly, because we're too scared to imagine being alone. Here's Marisol's story about how she had to walk away when she saw that her best friends had turned into anything but.

MARISOL'S STORY: "They didn't Even care that They were Hurting Me."

I'd been friends with the same group of girls since sixth grade, but when we got to high school, they started to act very different. There was another girl who joined our group who would do stuff that was really kind of horrible, like spit into people's food at lunch when they weren't looking—I think because it made my friends laugh. I could tell this girl didn't like me too much because I wasn't one of her followers. Pretty soon my friends were saying all kinds of mean things about people, including me.

I stayed around and took it for a while, because I still hoped that they would turn back into the friends they once were to me. I tried to talk to them about how they were acting, but they just stood there acting like what I was saying was funny. It was like another stab in the heart. I stopped calling or texting them, and it was like they didn't even care, which hurt me even worse. I was really upset and depressed after that happened. I'd see them in the hallways and they would look right through me like I didn't even exist. I eventually realized that even though I was sad, I also felt independent like I was free, you know! I hadn't realized how much their putting me down had been affecting my confidence until I took a step back from it.

For more about dealing with losing friends, see the question "What do you do when a friendship you've had for a really long time falls apart?"

Sometimes we have to find other ways to take away their power. Sixteen-year-old Suzanne uses a mantra that she repeats to herself whenever she's faced with mean girls. She explained, "Every time I walk past this group of girls in my school who make obnoxious comments about the way me and my friends dress, I just tell myself, *Don't let these bitches bother you. . . . Ignore them. . . . They are not better than you, even if they think they are!*"

You can even use a tangible symbol to remind yourself of what's beautiful and true about you, so their mean words can't get to you. Fifteen-year-old Latonya was tormented by a group of kids at school who yelled out cruel comments about her weight. At the workshop I'd done at her school, I gave out *Ask Elizabeth* heart-shaped gold lockets and had the girls put in a picture on one side of themselves when they were at their happiest, and on the other, a picture of someone they love who inspires them to be their best. Latonya told me later that she held that locket every time she walked by that group of nasty kids—that reminder of her own strength helped her stop their mean words from getting into her head or her heart.

ACTION STEP # 3

Reach Out for Help

It's not worth it to tell anyone at my school—they won't do anything about it.
It will just make the situation worse.
I'm too scared of what they'll do if I tell anyone.

If you're telling yourself any of these things, I know they feel very real, but please, please, please . . . if you do absolutely nothing else, I'm begging you: don't suffer in silence. I know you're probably feeling so lonely—like no one can possibly help or understand the pain that you're going through. But now more than ever, you need to seek out support.

Here's Rachel Simmons's advice on reaching out for help.

LEADERSHIP FOR LIFE author

ASK THE EXPERTS

Rachel Simmons on Asking for Help

The first thing I want you to remember is this: sometimes the thing that feels so right to do is actually the wrong choice. And not telling anyone about what you're going through is one of those wrong choices that can feel so right. Can you trust me on that? When you're alone, you hold all of the pain inside yourself. That pain can hurt you in deep, powerful ways that you might not even realize. It will make the process of coming out of this darkness longer and harder if you do it alone.

First, let's define "help." It comes in many forms. It might just mean having someone to listen to you. Just having a place to dump out your feelings can be a huge relief. Help can mean someone who hangs out and distracts you with a movie night or pickup soccer game. Help can also mean intervening. Take a minute to think about what kind of help feels right to you in this moment.

Now think about a person who could give you some help. I'm going to be straight with you and tell you that if you're suffering at the hands of a bully or abusive person, I think it's really important for you to tell an adult. Can you think of one person right now who you could talk to who would listen to you and respect your wishes: a teacher, a counselor, a relative, or a parent?

If you're not sure, you could approach this adult and say, "I want to talk to you about something I'm dealing with, but it's really important to me that you . . ." Then you say what you need up front: "I need you not to tell anyone else. . . . I need you just to listen. . . . I need some advice. . . ." Whatever it is, say what you need. Let the person tell you if they can respect your wishes. If they can't, that's cool. You didn't say anything yet, and you can move on and find someone else.

ACTION STEP # 4

Separate What They Say from What You Believe About Yourself

Not letting the mean things people say about us become what we believe about ourselves is one of the hardest things to do. But when you learn to do this, I swear, you will save yourself from so much suffering.

When you hear something over and over—whether it's good or bad—it's so normal to just take it in as fact, but it really is a conscious choice we make to let others be in control of our self-esteem. Just like we talked about in chapter one, it's within your power to take a step back from what they are saying, and remember that what you believe about yourself is up to *you.* If something they say hits a true nerve for you—like you're already down on yourself about your weight and they target you for being heavy—it comes back to all the tools we talked about in chapter one, to strengthen your inner reserve of self-esteem.

It took a long time, and lots of tears, love, and support from the people closest to me, to begin to heal from that time when it felt like I was being attacked from every direction. Mostly I had to look deep within myself and find a fierce determination to not let this derail me from my dream. Of course, there were moments when I thought, "Oh my God, are they right? Am I awful? Should I quit?" But in my core, I knew they were wrong. I wasn't going to let the onslaught of humiliation change my belief in myself or steal my passion for what I do--no way. Not an option. --xoe

I could have packed my bags and gone back to Michigan - Nope!

There's an inner fighter in all of us. If you haven't met yours yet, now's the time. She's in there, I promise! So dig down deep and find her, and make her your ally when you need her the most. This isn't about becoming hard or bitter—you don't need to be in fighting mode all the time. You'll know when she's needed.

I now know, deep in my bones, that other people's nastiness has absolutely nothing to do with who I am or what I'm capable of. That's the thought I hold when I feel a quick sting now after I hear or read something mean and have to get myself back on track. My BFF Seane has a great way of protecting herself from other people's negative stuff: she just says to herself, "Not mine!" Like a shield, it lets their nastiness bounce right off. And then she goes back to focusing on her own amazing strength and purpose in the world.

Or you can take the advice of fifteen-year-old Tanya, who definitely has the right attitude when it comes to refusing to let other people's mean comments bring her down: "Oh, I take it as a compliment. You got my name in your mouth? Then I must be important!" Love it!

ACTION STEP # 5

Use the Experience as a Source of Strength

I'm not saying this lightly, believe me!

It's been more than a decade, and I can now honestly say that as devastating as the experience I told you about was, it was a gift. Walking through that level of hell allowed me to find out what I was made of—and who I really am. Ironically, my character's name in the movie was Nomi, which over time came to symbolize to me how through this experience I came to "know me." And most important, the greatest gift the experience gave me was the inspiration to create *Ask Elizabeth,* so that girls everywhere could find their own inner reserve of strength, no matter what life throws at them.

I know that right now it might be hard to imagine that what you're experiencing will one day be a source of empowerment, so you might just have to trust me on this one. This *will* end, and you'll come through the other side wiser, stronger, and more compassionate for having been through it. And no one can take that away from you—ever!

What do you do if a friend is doing something that's really dangerous or bad for her?

You guys are such amazing friends to one another, so it's not surprising that I've gotten a lot of questions about how to help a friend when she's in trouble. You've talked about how scary it can be to watch someone you love do herself harm, whether through drugs, alcohol, cutting, an eating disorder, or even being in an abusive relationship . . . and how helpless and confused it makes you feel.

I talked to Suzanne Bonfiglio Baumann, an amazing teen counselor who works with high school girls in New York City and Boston. Here's what Suzanne wanted you to know:

"It can be really overwhelming to watch a friend hurting. Her feelings and behaviors can be really heavy for you—or even your whole group of friends—to carry alone. It's not just your friend who's hurting in this situation; you're struggling, too. You probably miss the way she used to be. In fact, she might have been the person you would have turned to in this situation; but now, she's in trouble and you're stuck figuring out a way to help her alone."

Seventeen year-old Carmen shared,

My friend started cutting herself after she got dumped by ~~the guy she liked~~ this guy she really liked. I found out because she would take pictures of her cutting ~~hers~~ herself, and I saw the pictures on her camera one day. It really shook me up. <u>Why</u> is she doing this?

I wanted to give you some understanding of a bit of the psychology behind self-destructive behavior and self-harm, to help you with any of the confusion. I asked Dr. Gail Saltz, who is one of the country's most respected psychiatrists and a bestselling author, to give us some insight into what your friend might internally be wrestling with. . . .

ASK THE EXPERTS

Psychiatrist • Columnist

DR. GAIL SALTZ

Bestselling Author • TV Commentator

on

Why Some Girls Harm Themselves

Intense sadness, worry, fear, and anger can be overwhelming, and some teens will turn to destructive behaviors and self-injury as a way to manage those feelings. Whether your friend is aware of it or not, she is having overwhelmingly painful feelings (sometimes even feeling empty and numb), and this is how she is distracting herself from those feelings. It feels like it works . . . for a little while, but the problem inside (the bad feelings) is still there, and even growing. So shortly, they do it again. If she's cutting, maybe the next time she does it deeper, harder. Your friend hasn't found another way to cope with her stress, sadness, and confusion, so she continues to hurt herself.

Okay, so now that you've got a little more understanding of what might be behind your friend's need to turn the pain on herself, what do you do?

Mind your own business or butt in (in a caring way). . . . That's what your decision here really comes down to, doesn't it? I hear you—you don't want your friend to hate you, but at the same time, are you supposed to just sit back and watch her go down a destructive path? I know with the huge heart you have, you already know your answer to that one. So how—and when—do you jump in and try to steer her in a safer direction?

Psychiatrist • Columnist • Bestselling Author • TV Commentator

ACTION STEPS: Helping a Hurting Friend

Of course we're going to give you the tools you need here, but first please hear me on this: *It's not your job to fix someone!* Your role as her friend right now is to support her in a loving way and/or to help get her to the next level of professional help she needs. Okay? Here are some steps to take to help your friend—sometimes one or the other step is needed, and sometimes both. . . . Each situation is different, and you'll have to use that smart inner radar of yours to know the right solution for you and your friend.

ACTION STEP # 1

Talk to Your Friend

It seems like the biggest fear you guys are up against is worrying that your friend will think you overstepped your bounds, which I totally understand. That's what makes this so tricky! As fifteen-year-old Michelle shared, "My best guy friend gets messed up at parties and then drives. . . . It scares me so much that he does this. One time I brought it up and he got so defensive and yelled at me, saying I didn't know what I was talking about. Since then I've been afraid to say anything, but I'm terrified that something really bad will happen."

When I'm in a delicate situation with someone I love and don't know what to do, I ask myself a very basic question: *What would love do?* Those words help me break through all the worries of, *What if she gets mad at me?* or *I'm not sure if it's any of my business.* Those worries are all totally legitimate, but they don't do us or our friends any good, right? When I know that I'm coming at the situation from a position of love and support, my fears of how she might not be happy with me fall away, and I feel more secure doing what I need to do for her.

Here are some stories and advice from girls about talking to a friend in trouble.

GIRLS TO THE RESCUE

How We HELPED OUR FRIENDS

elizabeth@ask-elizabeth.com >

Just recently one of my closest friends started getting into drugs and drinking. I asked her why she was doing this, and she said it wasn't a big deal, but when I pushed she teared up and said that the guy she liked was doing it so she felt like she needed to. I told her that she can do so much better. We deleted his number from her phone and got her away from him and from all the bad influences he brought with him. My advice is to try to get your friend to tell you why she's doing whatever she's doing, because then maybe you can help her with the real problem underneath. —Samantha, 17

From: < Caryn >

To: < elizabeth@ask-elizabeth.co

I think it's important to do something like this in private, so your friend feels safe. She'll probably get defensive at first, and you don't want to make the situation worse by adding public drama to it. —Caryn, 17

Even if she's mad now, trust me, later she won't forget how you helped her.

One of my best friends was starving herself. I couldn't sit back and not do anything, so I just said very calmly, "I love you, and I'm seeing what's going on, and I care about you too much not to say something. Will you please let me take you to the school counselor? I'll stay with you the whole time." I think having me go with her was the push she needed. —April, 15

Such a beautiful act of Support -- she'll know you're on her side

From: < Christine >

To: < elizabeth@ask-elizabeth.com >

I struggled in secret with depression for a long time. I'd put on a happy face for everyone, but inside I was dying. For the past two years, I've gone to weekly therapy, which has helped so much. But still, I wish I'd had a friend who I could have been honest with. I wish there had been someone who was willing to just step in and say, 'Hey, are you okay?' So if you suspect your friend is in trouble, just reach out and let her know you notice she's struggling.... She might need that more than you think." —Christine, 18

So many girls lives are turned around simply by admitting their problem to someone they trust.

I thought it might help to hear a story from a girl who deeply appreciated having her friend step in. Here's eighteen-year-old Risa's experience.

RISA'S STORY:

Subject: She Helped Me Wake Up to What I Was Doing

A few years ago I was bulimic. I didn't know I was. People kept saying, "You need help." But I was like, "I'm not bulimic. So what...I throw up a few times a day. Big deal."

A very good friend came up to me one day and handed me a big envelope. She told me that no one knew she was giving it to me, that it was completely between us. She said, "We don't have to talk about it. If you feel like you can trust me, call me and we'll talk."

I went home that night and opened the envelope. In it was a whole bunch of stuff she'd printed out from the Internet about bulimia. When I read it I broke down and was like, *Oh my God. I have an eating disorder.* I saw all the things in there that I'd been doing—flushers, pills, all of it. I didn't realize how much I'd been lying to myself and everyone in my life to cover it up.

I got hysterical for a lot of hours that night. When you see yourself in that kind of light, it's scary. I hurt so many people—pushed them away. Thank God for that friend. Seriously. Thank God. I love her more now than ever. That same night I went to this eating-disorders website that helps you figure out how far along you are in terms of being in danger, and I eventually got help.

Please see my website for resources for this.

If you have a friend who you think might have an eating disorder, write her a letter, or get information into her hands the way my friend did. Definitely let her know that no one else knows that you are communicating with her about this, because that's the main area of her shame (the secrecy). She needs to know that she can trust you.

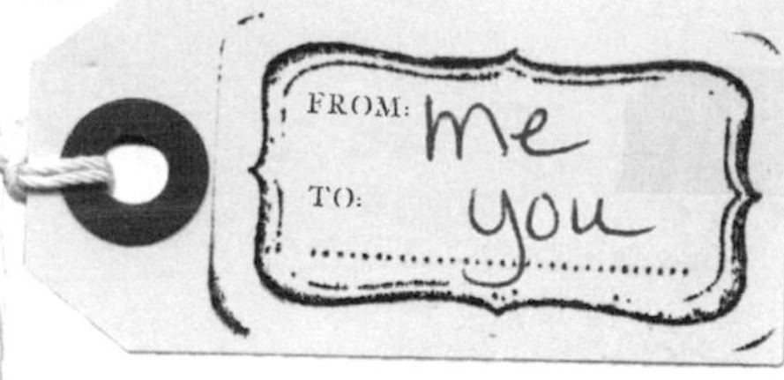

IT'S NOT PERSONAL

Some girls have told me that when they've discovered a friend's "secret" dangerous behavior, they take it personally that their friend didn't share it with them. This is not a sign that your friend doesn't love or trust you. She likely wasn't intentionally hiding it from you; she might have been in denial even to herself. Now's the time when she needs your compassion to help her with the deep shame and loneliness that stuffing down a secret like that might have made her feel. XOE

ACTION STEP # 2

Go for Help on Her Behalf

That's when taking this action step is an immediate must!

We can do our best, but the truth is that our friend might not be open to hearing us. Or she might pretend she hears us but then doesn't do anything to help herself. Or the problem might be bigger than something we're equipped to deal with on our own. As sixteen-year-old Alexis told us, "I got so wrapped up in trying to help my friend who was depressed, by being a shoulder to cry on, that I couldn't see that what she really needed was professional help. I thought that since we were so close I could help her, but there are some issues that girlfriends can't solve for each other."

So what do you do? Do you go to her parents? Again, I know you might be nervous because you don't want her to hate you, but no one I know has ever regretted stepping in to save someone's life. You can be there for her, support her, and offer her your love, but ultimately, when the situation is serious (and any situation where she's at risk is serious), you absolutely need to go to her parents, a guidance counselor, or another adult you trust.

Here's sixteen-year-old Zoe's story about getting help for her friend.

ZOE'S STORY:

"At First I Didn't Know What To Do"

I had a friend who was doing cocaine. I stayed quiet at first, mostly because I didn't know what to do, untill one day I saw her doing it in the hallway at school. This seemed OUTRAGEOUS to me, and so I organized an intervention with her parents. I'm not going to lie I was extremely scared she wouldn't want to be friends with me in the future. But in this situation it was necessary to put our friendship at risk in order to save her health. at first she did get mad, but I think in a way she was relieved that someone finally busted her. She went to rehab. and has been sober for nine months, and we're still good friends. I don't regret for a second telling her family, because this problem was beyond my control. You get to a point if you care about someone that maybe you have to do the hard thing, even if it means you might lose them. I love my friend and this was the best way I knew to help her... I couldn't live with myself if anything bad happened to her. If your friend is in serious danger, you have to go to her parents. Even if she says they won't care or she'll never speak to you again. She's probabely telling you that to prevent you from talking to them.

To me it's okay to cross a personal boundary in the ~~name~~ name of protecting someone's safety- wouldn't you agree?

Like we said in "If a friend hurts your feelings, how do you confront her without making her mad?" the reality is that your friend might, in fact, get angry or upset.

Don't worry, and don't second-guess yourself. Let me tell you: if you've been holding on to concern that your friend needs help, then it must be true. Do not let anyone convince you that you're being dramatic. In your heart, you know you did the right thing for her, and hopefully one day soon she'll see that, too.

ACTION STEP #3

Help Yourself

You are such loving friends to have your friend's back the way you do. And as you put these action steps into practice, I just want to make sure that you remember to also take care of yourself.

Because you care so much about your friend, what she's doing to herself affects you, too. You may not even realize that the time and energy you're spending worrying about her is consuming you, so check in with yourself on that when you find yourself in this supportive role. Suzanne says, "It may sound selfish, but your first responsibility here is to yourself. Be honest with yourself and ask, 'Is this too much for me to handle alone?' If your stress level is high (Are you having trouble sleeping? Is your friend's problem occupying your thoughts and distracting you from other parts of your life? Are you feeling anxious?), you might need to talk to someone yourself about what's going on within you."

I hope this gives you the permission to take care of yourself in the way that you need to if you're going through this. Please hear me on this: the best way that we can help someone we love is by being the strongest, healthiest version of ourselves. Even though your friend may be struggling right now, that's what she would want for you—and it's what I want for you, too.

WHAT DO YOU DO
WHEN A FRIENDSHIP
YOU'VE HAD FOR A
REALLY LONG TIME
FALLS APART?

(MY FRIEND ENDED IT)

When I read this question at a workshop, I almost started to cry myself. A few years ago one of my best friends, Ella and I were going through a really tense time. Our friendship was so precious because we shared a rare kind of closeness, but we'd been having lots of drama and difficult discussions, and then one day out of the blue, she dumped me by sending me a handwritten letter via FedEx. The only explanation she gave me was "It's better for me if we're not in contact right now."

Losing a friend can be as painful as any breakup with a guy, if not more so. . . . Girlfriend bonds run deep. I know some well-meaning people in your life might say, "But you have other friends," or try to minimize the pain you're feeling in another way, but I'm sorry, the reality is that losing a friend seriously hurts. When I got that letter from Ella, I felt an instant emptiness and loneliness. Who would I ever meet who would know me that deeply; who could I be that free and goofy with? She was the kind of friend who—with just one look from across the table—would know every thought in my head. For a long time I wondered how I was ever going to be okay without her.

Don't you hate when someone tells you you're overreacting?

You guys don't need me to tell you how many different ways and reasons friendships can break apart. So many of us have had some experience with this. . . .

"What do you do when a friendship you've had for a really long time falls apart?" (My friend ended it)

WHEN OUR BFF DUMPED US

RETURN TO SENDER

Over the summer my best friend became friends with this group of girls from her church. Suddenly she said I couldn't hang out with her or them anymore because I wasn't religious enough. She actually said I was a bitch. It was so hypocritical.

Gretchen 17

It's weird, but sometimes when someone is trying on a new identity, they run from anything that reminds them of who they were before.

To: < elizabeth@ask-el

Subject: My BFF Dumped Me

One day my best friend just stopped talking to me and stopped returning my texts. and then my whole group of friends went along with her. I don't even know what happened, and that's been the hardest part for me. It was a big hit to my self-esteem; I feel like now it's so hard to make friends because I'm afraid it will happen again...like there's something wrong with me...

—Katya, 15

My best friend started dating this guy, and she fully chose him over me. It was such a cliché move. I feel like she doesn't really doesn't care.....I've said I miss you, can we please spend some time together, and she just completely blows me off. I feel pathetic, like I'm this puppy dog running after her, trying to get her attention. —Zoe, 15

To: < elizabeth@ask-elizabeth.com >

A few months after my best friend in the entire world's mom passed away, she started to act strange around me. I thought she was just going through a tough time, but after a few months went by of her basically ignoring me, I got really upset, so I called her one afternoon to see if she needed to talk and see what was up. She flat-out said, 'I don't want to be associated with you anymore.' I tried calling and e-mailing her like twenty times after that, but she never answered—not a single word. —Carina, 16

Dealing with the Loss

I totally get why, in a moment like this, you'd start to question everything about yourself. Rejection can hit you where it hurts the most and kill your self-esteem, if you let it. But we're not going to let it!

Look, it's always good to first ask yourself honestly, *Did I do anything to cause this?* But if the answer is a flat-out no, then the best way for you to take care of yourself is to deal with the loss so you can heal. (Might be a good time to reread the section titled "How do you get over a broken heart?" This is heartbreak, the same as losing a love relationship!)

There's a saying I love that has saved me many times: "Rejection is God's protection." Good one, huh? It reminds me that even if I can't see in the moments of rejection why something is happening, I have to have faith that there's a reason why, and sometimes it makes the rejection a little easier to accept.

Like we've said before, there is always a hidden gift in every tough situation, even if it takes a little while to discover it. I didn't know at the time when I got that FedEx "breakup letter" from Ella that after the pain, I would eventually feel some relief and peace inside. Letting go of the drama that went on between us freed up huge amounts of precious time and energy we didn't even realize we'd been giving up to keep the relationship going.

Though I still don't think a FedEx letter is ever the right way to end a friendship!

Maybe for you, this friend (or friends) leaving your life is going to show you how the friendship had been holding you back in some way, the way it did for sixteen-year-old Cheryl, who said,

My girl Alexandra and I were like one unit, you know? We were together *all* the time. And when we had a big ~~fight~~ blowout and stopped talking, at first I was like, "This sucks... now I'm a total loser without any friends." After a few weeks, I started to see how much I'd always just let her decide where we'd go, what we'd do, that kind of thing. I don't think I ever saw how ~~much~~ passive I was being, or how I kind of thought I needed her 'permission' to do anything on my own. I lost her, but I found my opinions again.

If it was a hurtful betrayal, maybe this will open you up to find some new friends who are going to have your back. I know it might seem like there is no way that anyone will get you the way she did, but I promise you, you will find other amazing friends out there who not only get you but fully appreciate you for the incredible friend that you are.

In moments of rejection, trust that it will all make sense soon—even if right now it doesn't feel that way.

ACTION STEPS: Letting Go, Moving On

It's so normal to hope that your friend will turn back into the person you became friends with in the first place. Believe me, I spent a lot of time wishing that my friendship with Ella could have stayed the same as it was at the very beginning. As much as we hate it, though, people do change . . . and we change. Even if we do everything we can to fix the relationship, things don't always work out, and we have to move on for our own well-being.

Don't worry, I'm not going to just leave you hanging and just say, "Move on." You know me by now, don't you? We need some action steps here to help you pick up the pieces!

ACTION STEP # 1

Forgive Her...for Your Sake

I know, the idea of forgiving a friend who hurt you feels impossible, right? You're probably worried that if you do that, it's like saying the way she treated you is okay—and it is so not! It's never okay for someone to be mean-spirited. Fifteen-year-old Sadie talked about the kind of anger that's so normal to feel when we've been betrayed or hurt by a friend. She shared, "My friend Mia did the thing you're never, ever supposed to do to a friend: she got together with my boyfriend—while I was still going out with him. I found out they'd been messing around for months behind my back. I just get so pissed off every time I think about it. . . . It's eating me up inside."

Sadie's right: holding on to negative emotions like this can destroy us. Like we talked about in the question "How do you get over a broken heart?" even though we think that staying angry hurts the other person, the reality is that the resentment we have inside punishes us more than them. No joke, our emotions affect us physically—they can actually cause us to get sick from the stress and pain. Forgiveness doesn't necessarily mean you want to be friends again, or that you're excusing their behavior. You're just letting go of the anger for your own well-being. See the difference?

Here's how seventeen-year-old Theresa wisely put it: "It took me a long time to learn that everyone is flawed in some way, and that people are going to hurt you whether they mean to or not. Whenever you feel yourself getting hurt by what happened again, you have to remember that there is good in everyone and there is just something in them that is flawed that made them do it—insecurity, fear, whatever. Even though it's that person's fault that we're hurt, and even though they did what they did, it's our fault if we choose to hold on to our pain. It's okay to be sad, to talk about it, but there has to be a point when you say, 'This isn't going to continue to hurt me. I'm going to let go of this and move through it and work on making myself and my life better.'"

BTW, you don't need to make some grand gesture or even let your friend know you're forgiving her. You can just make an internal decision to let go and move on.

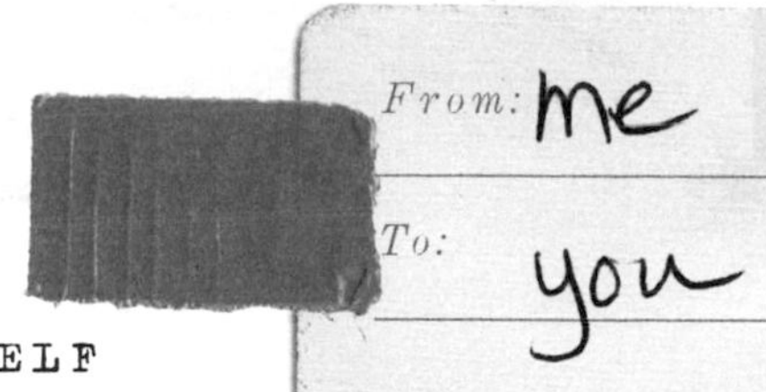

FORGIVE YOURSELF

Sometimes we lose a friend because of something we've done. When that happens, even though you might feel ashamed, it's important for your own self-worth to own up to your actions and do everything you can to fix the situation. And then, whether or not your friend forgives you, you'll need to forgive yourself. We're human, and we all make mistakes sometimes.

This doesn't mean you forget about it entirely. The takeaway gift here is knowing what you don't want to repeat. You get a reminder of how precious your friendships are, and why you want to be careful to protect them in the future. It's like, "Great...lesson learned. Got it!" XOE

ACTION STEP # 2

Embrace a New Reality

I'm not saying that the history you had with your other friend can be replaced by someone new right away—no way! Don't forget, that friendship took time, nurturing, experiences, and sharing to build it into what it was. Trust me, there were moments when I craved picking up the phone to call Ella because she knew me so well—there was such a shorthand there. But we're always changing and growing, and when a friendship comes apart, it can be an opportunity to make new friendships that are more authentic to who we are now, which is exactly what fifteen-year-old Julia did: "When we got to seventh grade, my three best friends suddenly got caught up with a crowd that was doing stuff I was definitely not comfortable with: smoking, texting naked pictures to guys, that kind of thing. They basically just left me behind. It was so scary and sad for me, because I had no one. I hadn't ever really thought to open myself up to new friends, but suddenly it was like I had this emptiness, and I realized that these girls from my tennis team were all really nice and so much more like me. It took a while to get to know them and feel comfortable, but it's two years later and these girls are now the best friends I could ever ask for. Oh, and my original group? So far, one has gotten suspended and all three of them have the worst reputations. I couldn't be more relieved not to have those girls in my life."

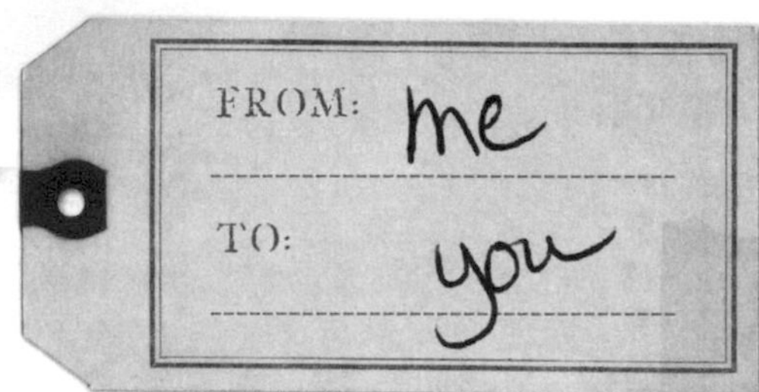

THE SECRETS TO MAKING NEW FRIENDS

Making new friends can definitely feel intimidating at first. But here are the three simple secrets from me and other *Ask Elizabeth* girls that can make it much easier:

* STAY REAL. Remember, no going into "wanting to please" mode! When you present who you really are, without trying to win anyone over, you'll attract more people into your life that you feel truly comfortable with.

* SEEK OUT LIKE-MINDED PEOPLE. Start doing activities that you love or have always wanted to do, and you are almost guaranteed to find people you're aligned with.

* CREATE CONNECTION BY OPENING UP. Revealing something personal about yourself invites the other person to do the same, which moves the friendship to a deeper level. When you start to feel like you can trust the person, take a small risk and share something, and you'll probably see that she does the same in return. XOE

Something small at first.

What if You're the One Who Needs to End It?

There's another side to this: what about the friendships that we need to get out of because we know they just aren't good for us anymore?

Ugh, the friend breakup—so not fun! The stories here are from girls who have been in that tough position of having to end a friendship that's not good for them. (BTW, you can find more ideas in the question "How do you know if you're in the right relationship?")

MARGUERITE'S STORY:

From: L

To: [elizabeth@ask-elizabeth.com]

Subject: I Didn't Like Who I Was Turning into Around Her

I had a friend named Shayna who was always horrible to people. When we became friends, she brought out the nastier person within me. I'm not blaming her for when I was mean to people, but I fell out with a lot of people because of this girl.

Even my mom said she didn't like me since me and Shayna had become friends; I'd started speaking in the same rude way that Shayna spoke to her parents. One day I overheard this boy I've known since I was twelve say to Shayna, "Before Marguerite met you, she was so cool, but since she's been hanging out with you, no one likes her."

I went home that night and cried and cried. . . . I couldn't believe who I'd turned into. Once I started to distance myself from her, of course she turned on me and started telling people private stuff about me. She was so brutal. I just kept telling myself that I was doing it to get back to the version of myself that I liked and respected. After about two months she forgot about me and moved on to her next "BFF," and believe me, I'm a lot more careful now about who I hang around with.

GENEVIEVE'S STORY: "I was staying friends with her out of guilt"

I had a friend from the time I was really young, and once we got to high school, she turned into this very clingy person and I felt like I couldn't breathe. She would get suspicious and jealous and mad anytime I did anything with someone else. I tried to talk to her about it, but she would always just break down and start crying. It was taking a huge toll on me.

Emotions are, of course okay but if you can't tell someone your feelings, that's not fair.

I talked to my mom about it, she told me that staying friends with someone just because I feel bad for her isn't helping either of us. I knew my friend would never let me just gradually distance myself, so I took her out to lunch and told her as nicely as I could, "I love you, but I think we've grown really far apart, and I think we should take a little breather from each other and see how things go."

She did her usual, starting to cry hysterically—I was really kind and got her some tissues, but I didn't take back what I'd said. I felt bad because I cared about her so much, but at the same time I felt relieved. She eventually found other friends, and I'm free from the guilt of having to take care of her all the time.

My advice to any of you who need to break up with a friend: if you are seriously contemplating ending a friendship, that means there's something wrong. And if you do end the friendship, don't let anyone convince you that you're too dramatic—it's something you needed to do for you, not anyone else. Also, stick to your decision. Don't be wishy-washy. Stay strong, because going back only means you'll have to go through the same thing in the future with her.

I get how heartbreaking it can be to let go of a friendship that was once meaningful to you. You want to hold on for dear life and do everything to keep it the way it was, right? But we can't continue a connection if we feel like it's forced, especially if it's one that's causing us pain. I think it's really important to let go of that friend—with love—when you sense that it's that time.

And with that love there, who knows. . . . The door is never closed when your heart is open. With some time and distance, you might find that you and your friend just needed to take a break from each other. Once you've both moved on to a new phase, you might come together in a new way. And yes, I'm saying this from experience!

Ella and I have slowly started to text and e-mail and share little things about our lives again. We've both expressed our gratitude for what the other has given us, and from there, who knows? Maybe there is space now to create something new. It definitely won't and can't be the same as what we used to have years ago, but honestly, we've both come so far in our own growth that we wouldn't want to go backward anyway.

I love how fourteen-year-old Monique views the passage of friendships. She said,

My mom once told me:

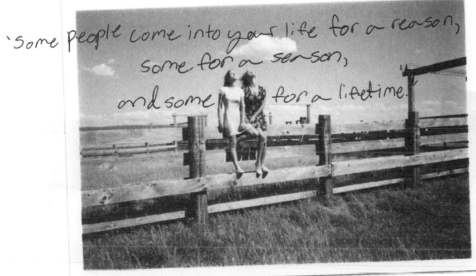

'Some people come into your life for a reason,
some for a season,
and some for a lifetime.'

Remembering that always makes it easier for me when someone I love leaves my life, because I know that not everything has to last forever in order for it to have mattered.

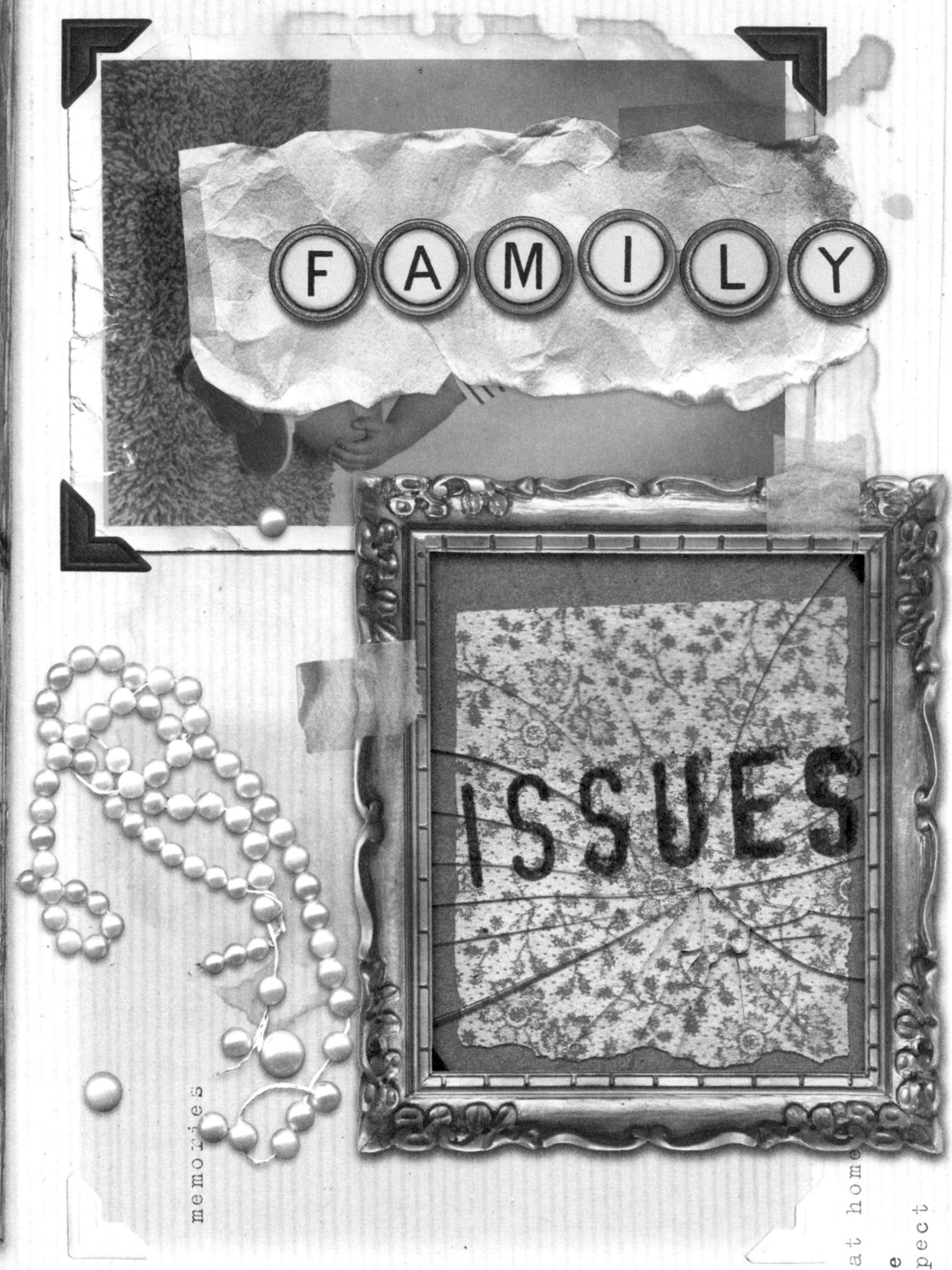
FAMILY
ISSUES
memories
drama at home
rememberance
respect
peace

drama at home
memories
communication
peace
4
remembrance
memories
...LET'S
TALK?!

DEALING WITH DRAMA AT HOME

* *

When it comes to parents, it seems like the biggest issue you deal with is communication.... Or I guess I should really say lack of communication. You want them to understand where you're coming from and to give you some space, and they want you to respect their rules, and in between is so much drama, right? The one thing you and your parents probably have in common is that you all want some peace.

In this chapter, you're going to get some ideas on how you can actually make that happen. I know you've been trying to do this on your own, but a girl needs some tools! There are actually ways to get you the space you want without having to go through crazy battles. Your *Ask Elizabeth* sisters and I are going to show you how to minimize the fighting. Wouldn't that be such a relief?

But as you know, family issues are about more than just getting along. There's also tough stuff like having to go through the terrible pain of actually losing a family member. We'll talk about that here, too, so we can get you the help and comfort you need.

So let's take a peek behind those closed doors and start making life better for you at home. What do you say... you in?

My parents treat me like a baby! How can I get them to give me more freedom?

I have no privacy. My phone has a code to lock it, but I know my mom checks it every night. She asks my friends for their phone numbers, and will call them if I'm out with them and don't pick up my phone. She's all over me... ALL THE TIME! -Inez, 15

My parents HARD-CORE baby me. It's lights out at ten, no more phone, no TV. At almost seventeen, that's getting to be TORTURE. There are seventh-graders who get to go to bed later than I do! - Sydney, 16

My parents came to this country when they were in their twenties, and they don't understand the culture here at all. They give me lectures about how I have too much fun, more than they ever had when they were teenagers, and so they keep me on a tight leash. ~Dara, 17

I hear a lot of you telling me that you're having similar feelings. You're not a little girl anymore, and you want to spread your wings and try new things without feeling boxed in. I also hear you telling me that your parents don't think you're ready for that level of freedom, and so you're understandably frustrated. Major power struggle! So how do we deal with this problem to get you what you want?

The Secrets to Negotiating More Freedom

Right up front, what we all want to give you is the single most essential factor in getting your parents to give you more space to do what you want. Ready? Here it is:

Drumroll, please! ☺

Honest communication + trust = freedom!

That's the key to all successful negotiations and this is a negotiation!

To put this into action, it helps to first understand where your parents are coming from. I've heard from a lot of moms and dads on this one, and, of course, from many of you, and here's what it comes down to.

First, they love you and want to protect you. As fifteen-year-old Michelle said, "Imagine the most precious thing in your life right now. Maybe it's your boyfriend, your best friend, or your dog. What if something were to happen to that thing? That's how it feels to your parents. They just want to keep their most precious thing close to them, to protect it."

Second, they're scared. You're changing, doing new and different things, and chances are, you're not telling them much about what you're up to. It totally makes sense to want your privacy; I get it. But here's the thing: if they don't know what you're doing or who you're hanging out with, they're left completely in the dark—worrying. And so they're reacting out of that fear and just saying NO across the board.

Here's where the honest communication comes in. It's a give a little, get a little kind of thing. When you start to tell them about even the small things that go on in your life, like maybe a party you went to, who was there, a funny story that happened with you and your friends, how you feel about something that happened in school . . . your parents feel less in the dark. They'll start to loosen their grip, because they know they can trust you, and because they're not so panicked that you're off doing dangerous secret things. See how it works?

Okay, so now that you've got that insight down, let's talk specifics . . . what you can do, say, etc., to be able to get that freedom you're so wanting. I'm going to turn this one over to your wise *Ask Elizabeth* sisters who have successfully paved the way. . . .

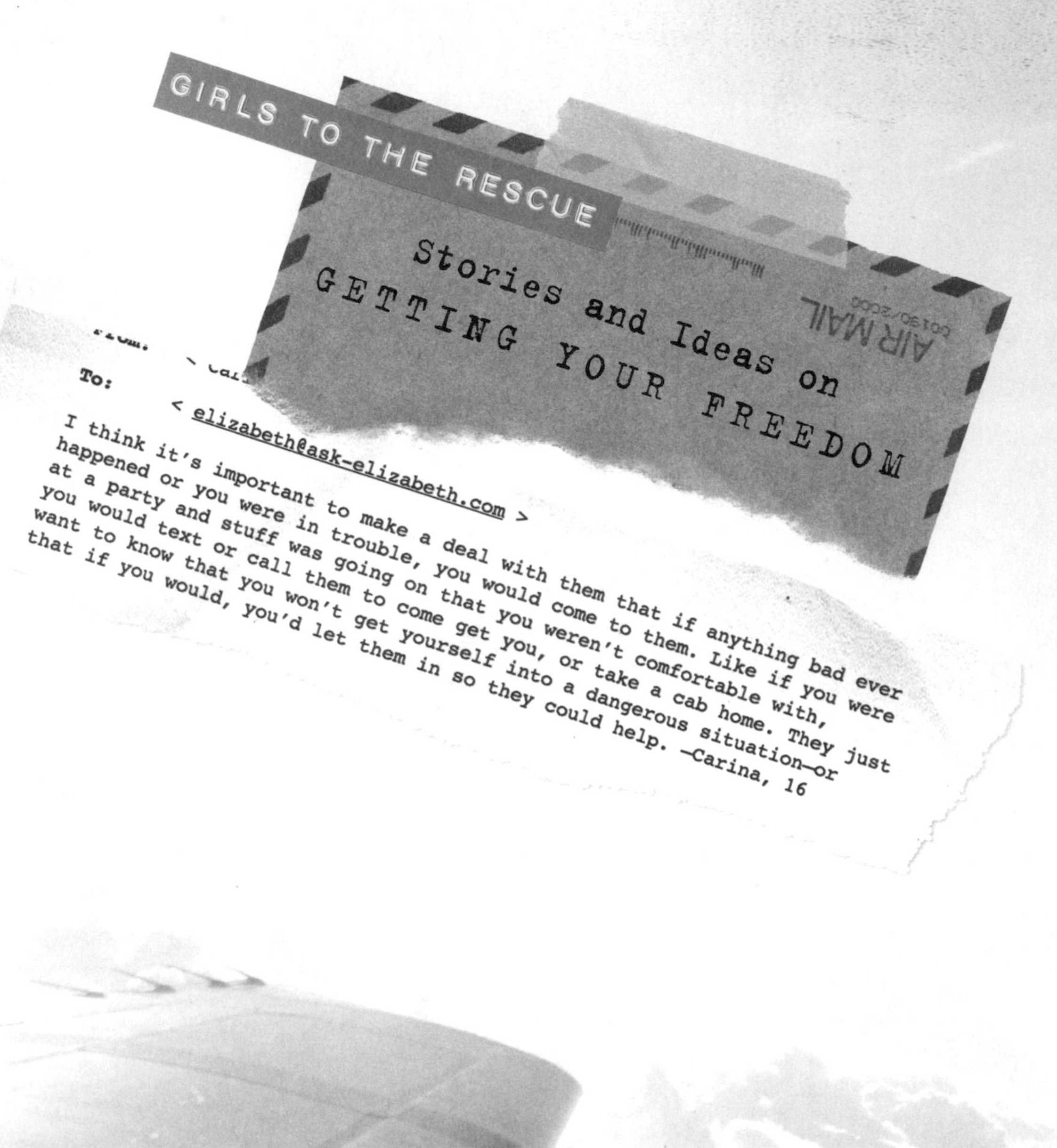

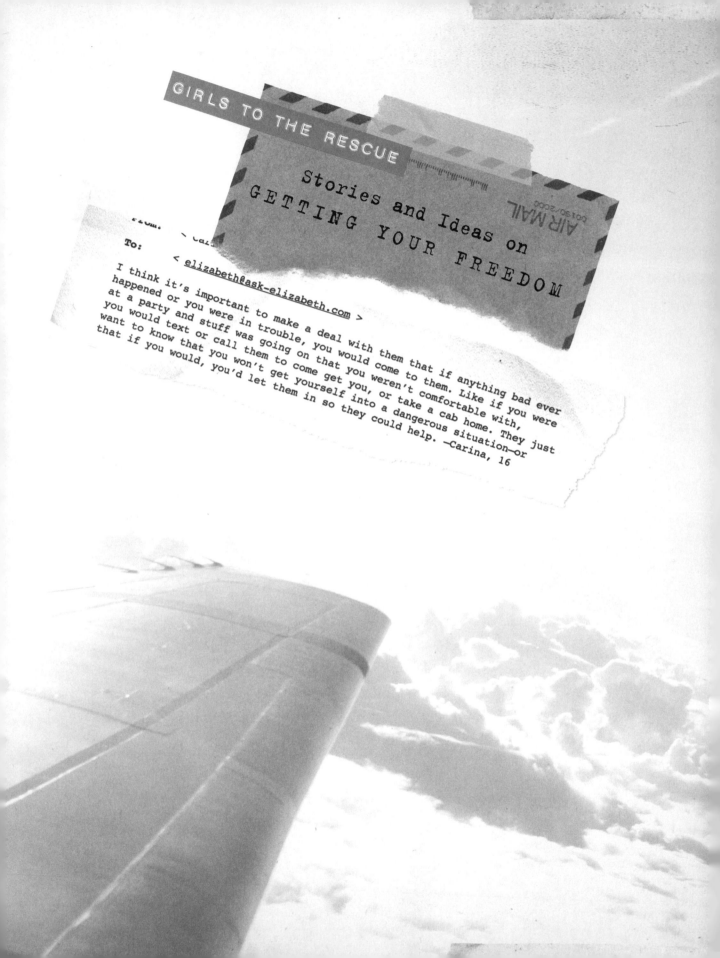

GIRLS TO THE RESCUE

Stories and Ideas on GETTING YOUR FREEDOM

From: < Ca

To: < elizabeth@ask-elizabeth.com >

I think it's important to make a deal with them that if anything bad ever happened or you were in trouble, you would come to them. Like if you were at a party and stuff was going on that you weren't comfortable with, you would text or call them to come get you, or take a cab home. They just want to know that you won't get yourself into a dangerous situation—or that if you would, you'd let them in so they could help. —Carina, 16

When I started helping my mom out with things around the house and following the rules, she realized I was becoming more of an adult and thus deserved to be treated like one. I showed her through my actions and not my words that I was capable of handling priveleges.

–Sharise, 16

To:

<ask-elizabeth.com >

I get 120% more freedom when I go out with my brother, who is two years older than me. If you have an older sibling, it helps to join in on their plans—that way, you have someone looking out for you and your parents feel better letting you do things. –Sasha, 15

This worked well for me, too... my brother Jason and I are so close and he is so protective, so it always made my parents feel good.

abeth@ask-elizabeth.com >

I guess maybe this is more of a story about what you shouldn't do: don't lie and say you're sleeping at your friend's house but really go to your boyfriend's. I got busted by my dad and now I'm not allowed to go anywhere. Don't be an idiot, because if you get caught, you've basically made it so much worse for yourself. –Frances, 17

To: iana

izabeth@ask-elizabeth.com >

When I got to the age where I wanted to hang out with guys, my parents really put on the brakes. I just sat them down and told them, 'Look, you taught me to be careful and smart.... You've got to trust that I've taken those lessons to heart.' Parents need to know that everything they've tried to drill into your head all those years actually stuck! –Iliana, 16

Don't shoot for the moon. If you know they are really strict, don't ask to stay out until three in the morning. Be reasonable! Maybe start by just asking for midnight, and then once they get used to that you can ask them to move it a little more. –Emmanuelle, 18

Step-by-step is good with strict parents – knowing who you're dealing with is smart negotiating.

< Mara >

To: < elizabeth@ask-elizabeth.com >

My mom used to ask me a thousand questions, and it drove me crazy. But then I just memorized the list of what she needed to know: who I'm going with, where I'm going, the apartment number if it's a party, etc. I just tell her these things and then she's fine. Get to know your parents' 'list.' If you don't know what it is, ask them. I'm sure they'll be more than happy to tell you! —Mara, 16

You've got to respect that you're changing the game on them. It's not like all of a sudden they're going to be like, "Hey, yeah, cool... Go do whatever you want!" You can't stomp your feet and whine. You want them to stop treating you like a baby? Then don't act like one!

– Chanel, 16

To: < elizabeth@a... >

Growing up, I was the baby in my family. I was always really close to my dad, and now that I'm in high school, I don't always want to be with him, and he won't accept that. The way I dealt with it was to make a plan to go to dinner as a family every Sunday night. That's when he gets to take me back as his baby, and as long as he has that, he's better. —Adanya, 14

Even parents need reassurance that they're wanted and loved!

From: < Jenny >
To: < elizabeth@ask-elizabeth.com >
Subject: Getting My Freedom

My mom has strict rules about how I dress: nothing above the knee, no cleavage showing at all, no spaghetti straps, nothing tight. I want to wear shorter dresses, tank tops, and some lower-cut tops. What I've been doing lately is (nicely) showing her pictures of other girls my age in magazines wearing the kind of clothes that I want to wear, so she can see that I'm just asking to be at the same level as other girls my age. She hasn't given in yet, but I can tell she's starting to come around.... —Jenny, 15

when i was a sophomore in high school, i got involved with a group of friends who were into some serious partying. my parents and i fought about this constantly. One night, two of my friends got killed in a drunk driving accident that they caused. it shook me up so badly, and all i could think was, That could have been me. That's when i finally got that my parents weren't trying to make my life miserable. They were trying to keep me safe.

Sarah, 16

By the way, just a heads-up: your parents will still act like your parents and be protective, even when you're out on your own. Just last week, my husband was away and I went out to dinner with my parents, and when we were leaving, my mom said, "Just text me when you get home so I know you got there okay." Cute, right? The world is so nuts, and they just want to know I'm safe. And if they need that, I'm happy to send that little text. Three seconds of typing in exchange for their peace of mind? It's a no-brainer.

Okay, so now you're armed with the tools you need to be a brilliant (and graceful) negotiator. Good luck!

My mom and I
don't get
along anymore...
All we do
is fight.
Is it going to be
like this forever?

Well, right up front, I actually have a quick answer for you: no, it won't be like this forever!

Does knowing that make what's going on in your house right now any less frustrating? Probably not . . . but at least you know from the get-go that there's a peaceful end in sight to the war that's going on between the two of you. → which is probably what it feels like to you.

I know I'm blessed to have an amazing relationship with my mom. She's my biggest cheerleader, the person I go to when I need advice or just someone to listen to me without judging, and my best girlfriend in the world. But don't get me wrong: of course we fight sometimes. Most of the time it's because I get mad at her for offering her opinion when I haven't asked for it. Just a look I see in her eyes or her silence in a moment when I'm telling her something can set me off, even though she was simply listening and being supportive. It's like, "*WHAT?* You don't agree?"

It's so crazy how we can love our moms so much and still have friction between us. There's just something about that mother/daughter connection, isn't there?

ACTION STEPS: Getting to Peace

Whether you feel like your relationship with your mom is a little rocky or a flat-out disaster, we're here to arm you with real-life strategies for taming the tension, putting out the fires, and creating parental peace. You don't have to do everything on this list; by putting even just one action step that feels doable to you into practice, you'll start the energy moving in the right direction.

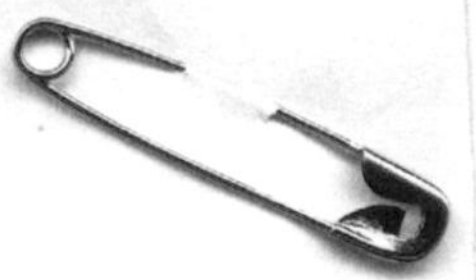

ACTION STEP # 1

Declare a Truce

"But she _______."

"If she wasn't so _______, then I'd be more _______."

"It's not my fault. . . . She's the one who _______."

I know, I totally hear you. Some of you have asked how you can possibly even consider declaring a truce when your mom does all those things that drive you completely *insane.*

Here's how: by really getting that change starts from within you. You're reacting to what she does, she's reacting to what you do, and you're both locked in this roundy-round of blame, anger, and frustration. You're thinking that it wouldn't be like this if only she would stop doing _______, but like we already know, we can't force someone else to change. Instead of waiting or hoping for things (or for her) to be different, we need to take control of the situation by being willing to change our own actions.

So let's just make a pact between all of us: no more drama! Who needs it? We need to fully make the decision of "No more . . . I don't want things to continue like this" in order to really be able to change things.

Take it from fifteen-year-old Miranda: "My mom and I would always fight, slam doors, and scowl—it was a never-ending battle over every little thing. And then I'd text my friend or we'd have these marathon 'You'll never guess what my mom did this time' conversations. It got to be like a sport—like we would compete to see who could give the best story. However, once I got over the allure of having 'mom issues,' I realized I was actually really tired of all the fighting. That's when we started to finally talk and worked together to try to have a peaceful relationship."

ACTION STEP # 2

Avoid the Triggers

You can save yourself so much stress by identifying the triggers that launch fights between you and your mom—and then doing your part to *not set them off.*

Let's say you know your mom goes nuts whenever your room is a mess. You hate cleaning up—I know, it's annoying. But let's be real: if your mom comes home and finds your room a disaster zone, you can't be surprised if she flips out on you! That's a fight you can easily prevent. Like Albert Einstein said, "Insanity is doing the same thing over and over again and expecting different results."

Good one, right? :)

Trust me, practicing give-and-take like that will give you a lot of relief. If you think about it, it takes a lot more effort to argue than it would take to bend a little, or to clean up your room, or to stop texting during dinner, or whatever else it is that sets her off. Think of it like a video game: instead of how many levels you can get to, the challenge here is: How many fights can you personally prevent?

ACTION STEP # 3

Tell Her (Specifically!) What's Bugging You

Some of you say you feel like you're from a totally different planet than your mom.

A lot of you have talked about feeling like your mom doesn't understand where you're coming from, or that she doesn't respect what you have to say. I had a conversation with an incredible group of girls at a school in North Carolina, and we had a breakthrough there that I think can help. Here's what we realized.

Especially if it's something really intense.

Because things get so heated when we fight with our moms, a lot of the time the frustration escalates and we'll scream things like, "You never let me do ANYTHING!" or "That is SO not fair!" I get that you feel that way, but here's the problem: we're not really telling them anything. We're just venting . . . which at the moment feels good, but we're in this to change the dynamic, right? And the way to do that is to actually communicate *specifically* what it is that's upsetting

Dear Mom,

As a daughter, I see you through your

you, so you can give her a chance to change it or clarify her side. I know you might be thinking, *But Elizabeth, she'll never change.* But wait . . . just trust me, okay? I'll show you what I mean.

Sixteen-year-old Stacey said that her mom just says no whenever Stacey asked to go out with her friends. Stacey would feel boxed in and ask why not, and her mom would yell back, "Because I'm your mom and I said so." That would make Stacey even more angry and frustrated, and then they'd spiral into yet another fight.

Stacey believed the rules in her house were okay when she was a kid, but now she felt she deserved to be given the chance to discuss the situation. So the next time it happened, Stacey calmly told her mom that she respected her rules, but being told "No, because I said so" made her feel like she was being treated like an immature kid, and that she'd like to understand her mom's real reasons for saying no.

Her mom heard what Stacey was saying (not screaming!), and explained that she was saying no for a reason Stacey didn't know anything about. Her parents were stressed about money and were trying to cut back on any unnecessary spending, including extras like movies, meals out, etc. So Stacey and her mom worked out a plan: she would use the money she earned from her part-time job when she wanted to go out with her friends—a compromise they never could have reached if Stacey hadn't been able to break through the unknown of "Because I said so."

So here's your new tactic: *be specific*. You already know all the reasons it's so important to communicate to someone you love about what's bothering you. When it comes to parents, it's good to really make sure we're being *super-specific* so we don't just end up in another screaming match of accusations and anger that goes nowhere.

I want to share an approach with you that worked really well with a mom and daughter I worked with in New York City. They loved each other so much, but the daughter, Madison, was feeling like her mom expected her to be perfect and that she was always failing in her mom's eyes. There were a lot of fights about grades, the clothes Madison wore, etc., but they all ended up sounding the same, with Madison yelling, "You don't even know me!" It was really tough for her, because she felt like her mom wasn't listening to anything she was saying, and it was

with conversational questions, so that we dont

need to, or feel like we have no one to talk to.

tough for her mom, too, because she felt alienated from her daughter. Here's what we did that worked great for Madison, and that you might want to try.

Since Madison and her mom could barely have a conversation without it turning into a screaming match, Madison and I decided that writing a letter was a good idea. This way, she could fully express herself, and her mom could take in the information when she had the time to fully focus on it. I sat with Madison and got her started on her letter. I told her to first vent everything she really wanted to say—to just let it rip. She just needed to get out all the anger and resentment first. Then we tore up that draft into lots of tiny pieces, so no one could ever read it.

Dont worry, this isn't the one she gave to her mom. Remember the goal is peace.

After that, we wrote a new letter with everything that she specifically wanted to communicate, including a few ideas which might also work for you.

* RIGHT OFF THE BAT, EXPRESS THE LOVE AND GRATITUDE YOU FEEL TOWARD YOUR MOM.

This is a great way to draw her in and let her know you're coming from a place of love. Madison told her mom how much she loved her and appreciated how she inspired her to aim high. See how that sets the tone?

* SHARE THE THINGS YOU HAVE BEEN FEELING HURT OR ANGRY ABOUT, AND HOW YOU WISH THEY COULD CHANGE.

Madison told her mom that her mom's expectations for her felt like a lot of pressure, and that she would appreciate it if her mom could see her for who she really is and not how her mom wished she could be (as in perfect).

* GIVE HER A VISION FOR HOW YOU WANT IT TO BE.

Madison felt like they hadn't made any fun new memories in a long time, so she wrote, "I miss the good times we used to have when I was younger, like when we would drive to ballet together and just laugh and catch up on fun life stuff, and I would love to do new things like that so we can get close again."

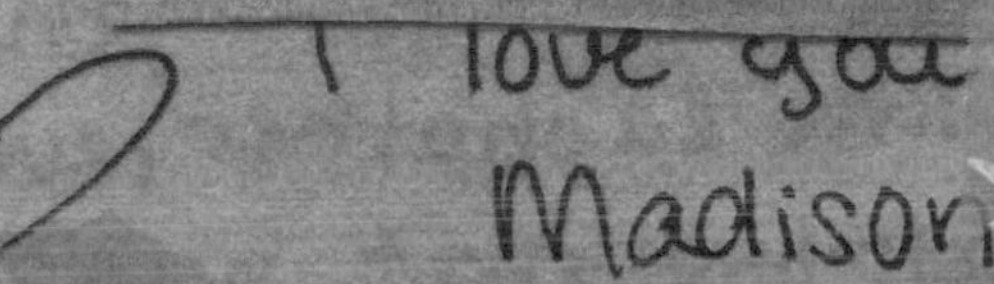

Whether you decide to write a letter or to tell her directly, expressing to your mom *exactly* what's been bothering you gives her a chance to do her part to change the dynamic between you. I'm guessing she doesn't love the fighting any more than you do!

ACTION STEP # 7

Defuse the "Criticism Bomb"

You know the kind of bomb I'm talking about:

"That outfit makes you look cheap."

"If you keep eating like that, you'll never lose the weight."

"Why can't you be more like_______?"

One comment like that from her and *BOOM*—the sparks are flying, right? Criticism (or what feels like criticism) from our moms can set us off like nothing else.

I know that it might not always feel like it, but our moms' intentions usually are good. They want to love and guide us, or sometimes even to save us from painful experiences they went through. They're trying to help us improve how we look, behave, sound, walk, talk, and make choices, so we can blossom into our best selves. But that still doesn't mean it feels good to be criticized.

So how do we stop that from happening? By teaching our moms how to communicate with us in a better way. Your mom isn't going to stop wanting to help you grow and shine. But that doesn't necessarily mean she can't learn to change how she's going about it.

Trust me, you still want that!

Here's how it works: let's say your mom says something like, "Your face is all broken out. . . . You need to be taking better care of it." Your first reaction is probably to get annoyed, right? But what if, instead of flipping out on her, you tried this:

Umm... like you don't have a mirror!

* Take a breath. (This stops you from snapping.)
* Connect to why she's saying that. (She loves me, wants me to look and feel good.)
* Tell her how you felt when she said that (upset, embarrassed, etc.).
* Suggest how she could communicate her intentions better.

So it would look something like this:

Mom: Your face looks so broken out again. You need to be taking better care of it.

You: [Take a breath.] Yes, I know, and I know you're saying that because you care, but it makes me feel really self-conscious when you point out how bad my skin looks. Maybe next time you could just tell me some ideas you have that might help? That would make me feel like you're on my team instead of trying to bring me down.

Criticism Bomb Defused!

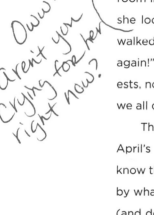

Owww... aren't you crying for her right now?

Here's a story from an *Ask Elizabeth* sister who wanted to show you this in action. Seventeen-year-old April was in tears as she told us a story about going prom-dress shopping with her mom. When April came out of the dressing room in the dress that she knew was "the one," her mom immediately told her she looked fat in it. April understandably got upset, took off the dress, and walked out of the store, yelling at her mom, "I'm never doing anything with you again!" Her mom very well might have been looking out for April's best interests, not wanting her to wear something that wasn't flattering to her body, but we all decided that how her mom went about it was definitely not okay.

The other girls in the workshop and I came up with a plan. The next time April's mom was critical of her like that, she would say something like, "Mom, I know that you want the best for me, but maybe you don't realize that I feel hurt by what you said." After that, she would show her mom how she would prefer (and deserved!) to be talked to. She could say, "Mom, I appreciate your input, which is why I invited you to come, but I would have rather you said something like, 'I liked the cut of the other dress you had on—I think it was more flattering.' That would feel better to me than putting me down."

See how it works?

ACTION STEP # 5

Find Ways to Bond

Fifteen-year-old Angela discovered another key to mom-daughter harmony: "My mom and I have a good relationship because we feel like we actually know each other as people, not just mom and daughter."

You already know that the more you open up to your mom about the things you feel comfortable sharing, the more connected to you she'll feel. And a closer connection means more peace for both of you. Besides sharing what's going on in your life, I love the idea of asking your mom about *her* life. Believe it or not, she was a teenager once, too! Even though it might seem a little uncomfortable at first, asking her to tell you about experiences she's had, stories about people she's loved, or challenges she's been through can be a major bonding experience for the two of you.

Not to mention that you might be surprised. Eighteen-year-old Katya explained, "Moms can be really cool—it's like they have a secret identity or something. I just learned the whole story of how my mom and dad met and fell in love—and that my mom was actually dating someone else when they met and she had to choose. It helped me see that she actually knows what she's talking about when she gives me relationship advice."

Here are a few other suggestions from girls about how to create more closeness with your mom.

GIRLS TO THE RESCUE

How to Bond with Your Mom

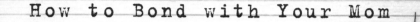

From: < Andrea >

To: < elizabeth@ask-elizabeth.com >

Doing a specific activity together every week or month is a great thing to do, so you can focus on something together other than your problems. You could take a yoga class or volunteer for a charity together. Your mom will probably be thrilled that you're making the effort. She might not even realize that you want to hang with her. —Andrea, 14

Moms usually love to give advice, so maybe start by asking her for advice about something that's going on in your life. She'll be *so* happy. She probably won't stop asking about it, which might be annoying, but it does feel good that she's interested. – Ellie, 16

From: < Theresa >

To: < elizabeth@ask-elizabeth.com >

My parents are divorced, and I spend half the week with my dad; I know it's hard on my mom, since my dad is remarried and there's this other mother figure in my life. So I try with my mom to just ask for her help with little things, like I'll say, 'Mom, can we look through these magazines together to find a new hairstyle for me?' or whatever, and I noticed that really helped our relationship. Moms just need to know that you still need them. —Theresa, 17

To: < elizabeth@ask-el

Try to find things that you and your mom have in common. My mom and I both love sappy love movies, so that's our thing. Trust me on this: rent the movie *The Notebook* with your mom. It's a total tear-jerker. That'll loosen things up! —Jin, 15

ACTION STEP #6

Open Your Heart

When I was talking to a group of girls at a workshop in Chicago about how they were all dealing with problems with their moms, a senior named Jessica told us a story that she and I want to pass along to you, because I think it can remind us of something really important.

me and my mom argue, like every mother and daughter do. I think I've had every single fight with my mom that you guys have talked about. but recently I had something happen that made me want to make things better between us. my best friend's mom was diagnosed with cancer and was given a few months to live. when I found out, the first thing I did was go home and just walk over to my mom and hug her. she was totally surprised—we just weren't like that. but that news really made me appreciate my mom, because I realized that she won't be around forever. that made me really want to put an effort into avoiding unnecessary arguments with her and ticking her off for no reason. fighting over getting to stay out later on friday night is nothing in the bigger picture.

I'm not saying that fights and disagreements won't happen. They always will, and that's normal. Oh, please—my mom and I still get into it now and then! Even so, you can love her, appreciate her, and understand that she's probably doing the best she can. As seventeen-year-old Hope said, "It's hard to remember that your mom's a person, too. She has feelings, and a life, hopes, dreams, failures, and all kinds of stresses you probably don't even know about. You have to remind yourself of that. She deserves your compassion and your love, the same as you would ask from her."

If your heart feels closed—like you are so tensed up that you can't even imagine feeling anything but anger toward her—you can try what always works for me when someone frustrates me: practice gratitude. Just sit down with a pen and a piece of paper and write what you appreciate about her. Trust me, it's hard to feel angry and grateful at the same time—and gratitude almost always wins.

Or email or text yourself a list—whatever works

Just like every other relationship we've talked about, the one between you and your mom will have good times and challenging times. Sometimes the people closest to us are the ones who test us the most. Like I told you, my mom and I still argue sometimes, but we've had a lot of practice over the years getting to know how to handle each other. Just keep working the action steps, and remember how much your contribution can change the dynamic for the better. You and your mom love each other . . . and that kind of love can get you two through anything!

And because we feel so close to them, we might feel more comfortable snapping at them.

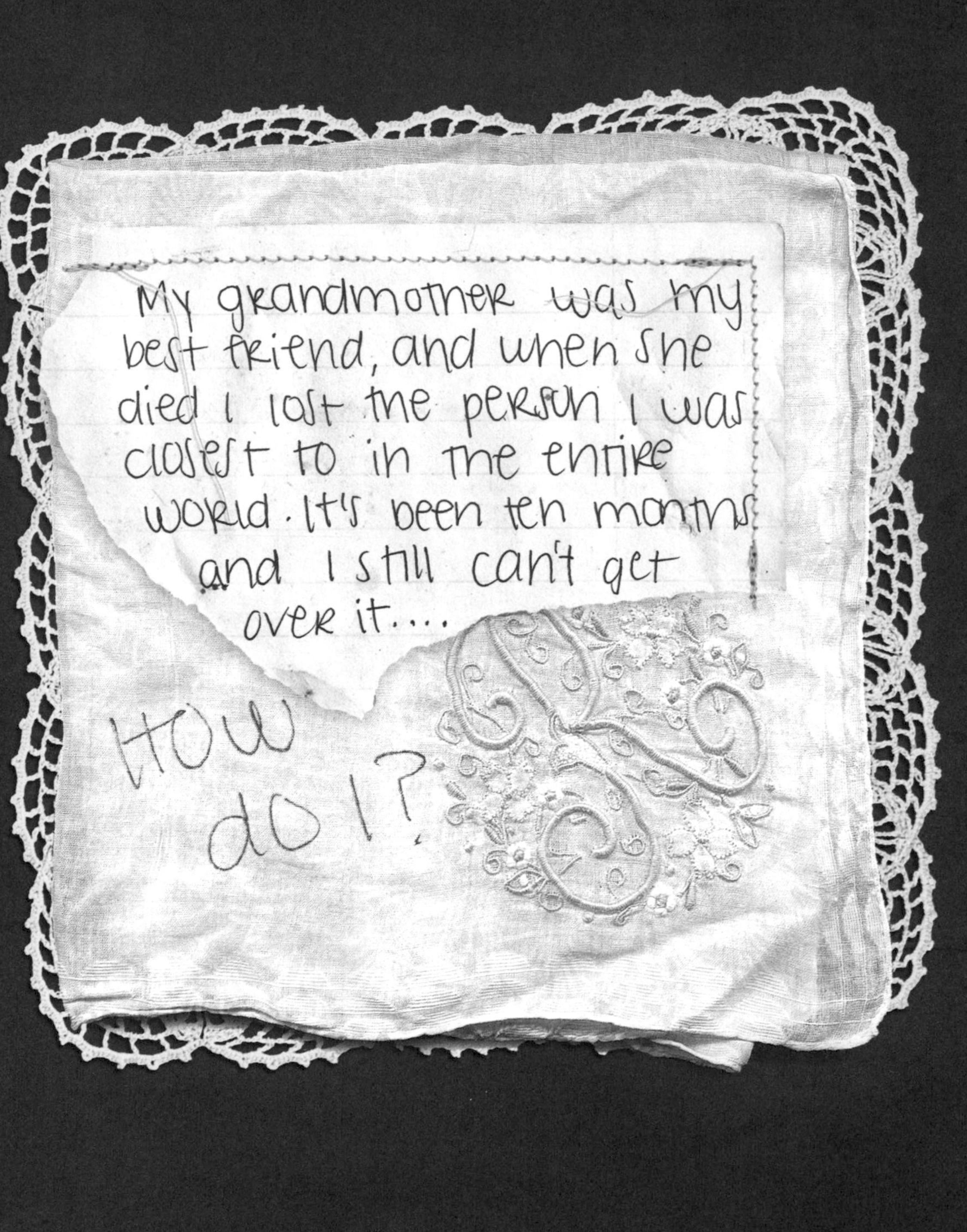
My grandmother was my best friend, and when she died I lost the person I was closest to in the entire world. It's been ten months and I still can't get over it....
How do I?

"CARPE DIEM."

Have you ever heard that saying? It means "seize the day," and it was my godmother Sherry's favorite mantra. Most people think carpe diem has to do with actual accomplishments, but she meant it more in terms of deeply feeling life's meaningful, rich moments. So she'd say it when we were laughing hysterically or even when I was calling her crying about a heartbreak, as if to stop and acknowledge, "Wow, we're really <u>in it</u>, aren't we?" I'm so grateful that she taught me to live that way, though I don't think I really got the full meaning of how important it really was until five years ago when Sherry died.

We met for the first time when I was five years old, and Sherry dropped off a big, red, heart-shaped box of chocolates on Valentines' Day for me from her son (he was also five at the time...my first crush!). Little did I know that that symbolic moment of her bringing a heart to my doorstep would be the beginning of an amazing journey and friendship. Just like the chocolates in that heart-shaped box, we devoured every moment of sweetness when we were together.

I was standing in my office in New York City when I received the e-mail from her husband saying that she'd died. I literally dropped to the ground.... It was as if my whole universe collapsed right along with me. If you've lost someone you love, I'm imagining you know exactly what I mean. --XOE

I can speak to you about loss not only because of what I went through losing Sherry; I've also lost other dear people in my life, and each time it's equally excruciating. My beautiful mother-in-law, Susan . . . my precious Granny . . . I hate that I have a list of lost loved ones. Doesn't it feel like we were robbed somehow, like they were stolen from us? We're mourning the loss of them but also the loss of all of the memories and experiences that *could have been,* and that makes the losses even harder to accept.

Let's gently look together at what you're feeling . . . okay?

The Process of Grief

You're hurting, and you wish you could know when it will stop, right? I'm so with you. It would be such a relief if someone could give us a timeline of how many days, weeks, months it will be until we start to feel better.

Unfortunately—and I think you know this deep down—there's no guaranteed timeline or formula for grieving. It's a process, and you have permission to let it be just that. Sometimes it's like two steps forward, one step back. Seventeen-year-old Kathy described her experience this way: "You go through some times when it hits you really hard, especially at the very beginning. And then it hits a climax, and you're kind of okay for a little while . . . until the next thing reminds you of them and you start crying all over again. It's like a roller coaster."

Please hear me on this: *it's okay to feel whatever you're feeling, at whatever pace you feel it.* People around you might say things like "Stay positive," or praise you when you're having a "good" day. I know that can make you feel like you aren't allowed to have the sad days, but you are. Even though their intentions are good, they might not always say the right thing, or the topic of death might scare them, especially if they haven't dealt with it before. It might just be hard for them to see you in pain, so they're rushing in to make it "better"—which just feels like more pressure to get over it quickly, right?

I love fifteen-year-old Kara's advice about this. She said, "I think my friends just didn't know how to deal with it when my mom died, and they just kept saying things like 'You'll get over it' or 'You're doing great.' For girls going through this, I think it helps to ask your friends to just listen . . . not for them to try to fix it."

The bottom line is that this is your process of grief, to feel and move through in your own way and time. Some of us feel it deeply right away, and that's how we heal, like sixteen-year-old Aviva. She shared, "My grandmother was an incredibly inspiring person—we were very close. When she died, I went numb. I tried to be sad, but I just wasn't. That is, until the funeral. I was standing in the front row and completely broke down, thinking about how I would never see her again, hear her laugh. I was practically hyperventilating. I cried like that on and off for two days, and then a kind of peace came over me at the thought that she wasn't hurting anymore (she could barely walk or breathe) and is in a better place."

Others of us need more time—a lot more time, and that's absolutely okay. Seventeen-year-old Ileanna shared her experience with that. . . .

ILEANNA'S STORY:

"It Was Like Being Stuck In A Bad Dream"

When i started Middle School, i was scared and lonely, until i met Gisele. For the next five years of my life i had the sister i always wanted. Then one cold February night, with one simple phrase my world came crumbling down: "**Gisele DIED.**" Hit by a car while crossing the street. It was so simple, yet so final. Why, now, why me, why my Gisele? i was numb, then sad and confused, then angry, and then all these feelings combined. i started losing **faith** in G-D and in **life**. i tried to replay the situation over and over in my head, like that could change the outcome. i felt my soul being ripped from inside me. i was **lost**, drowning in an ocean of my own tears and sadness, with no clue which direction to swim to find some level of **Relief**.

After months of being depressed and sleeping and seeing a psychiatrist, i started to realize i was **wasting** my life. If Gisele had been here to see it, she would have kicked my butt so hard that i would have been too scared to stay like that. But she wasn't, so i did it for **myself**. Some days were hard, some were easy, but either way i knew it had to be done. i started to make friends, i got a job, and slowly but surely my life started up again, like starting the engine of a car, for the first time in months.

"My grandmother was my best friend, and when she died I lost the person I was closest to in the entire world. It's been ten months and I still can't get over it.... How do I?"

It's been eleven months and twenty-seven days since Gisele died. im coping as best as i can, and everyday i learn how to deal with it better. The greatest thing i learned from her was to **live life** for **yourself** and not care about what others think about you.

Our friendship might have been cut short, but it was definitely sweet, and those memories are what continue to **heal** me. Because of **her**, i believe in Angels.

It's beyond lonely when you realize that there's no way to hug this person ever again, or talk to them or kiss them; I so understand that sheer, raw pain you're feeling that hurts like nothing else. Just allow yourself to do what you need to do as you're going through this. One minute you might need to cry hysterically, and the next you might need something light and happy to give you a little relief. Sometimes being alone when I'm missing someone really deeply is exactly what I crave; I just let my mind get quiet and think about what that person meant to me. Some people find grief groups tremendously helpful (for more on finding one, see the Pink Pages on www.ask-elizabeth.com), and other people turn to prayer. By now you know how to get what you need, because you're an *Ask Elizabeth* sister yourself, and we know how to take care of ourselves.

HEALING TOOLS: Dealing with the Pain

How do you make sense of it all and go on with your life without this person?

This isn't something we can give you a quick answer to, though you know that if I could take away your pain, I would do it in a heartbeat. Just like we talked about in the section about getting over a broken heart, the healing tools here aren't meant as a direct road map; you can use them in whatever order and as often you need to.

Keep Their Presence Close

I really do believe that love doesn't die. That energy you shared with someone is too powerful. Yes, the body goes, but that spirit that made them who they are and that spark of love and light can be with you always, and you can tap into it at any time in your quietest moments of thought or prayer, when you really need it.

Here's seventeen-year-old Nara's story of how her mom's energy is still such a huge presence in her life.

NARA'S STORY:

To: < elizabeth@ask-elizabeth.com >

Subject: **It's Like She's Just Always There with Me**

That whole first year after my mom died was pretty much about crying. And then after the first year, it became about accepting the fact that I couldn't change what had happened. I started thinking about how even though she wasn't with me physically, I'd always have her in my heart.

My mom left me her journals of me as a baby, and in them she wrote all these things that I would be going through in my life, like falling in love and problems with friends. She wrote to me that I'd see her again—and I do, in my dreams. One day when I was going through a particularly hard time I remember standing in my room, looking at a framed picture of my mom, wishing she was there...and then her picture fell and I saw that on the back that she wrote, "I love you, I'll always be there for you." And in all these ways, she is.

I see now that death is just a continuation of life. It's the next door, the next room. So even if they're not there with you physically, they're always waiting for you right in the next room. Embracing that helps you believe that they are still with you and know that everything is going to be okay.

Keeping someone's presence close to you can give so much comfort. Doing an activity that you used to do together—or even trying something that person loved—can make you feel that connection. Like if they loved gardening, you could plant their favorite flowers in your yard in their memory. My grandfather was a big believer in my dreams and used to come watch my tap-dance classes all the time, so whenever I put on my tap shoes, it's like he's with me. See what I mean?

"My grandmother was my best friend, and when she died I lost the person I was closest to in the entire world. It's been ten months and I still can't get over it.... How do I?"

HERE ARE SOME OTHER IDEAS YOU CAN TRY TO KEEP A CONNECTION TO SOMEONE YOU'VE LOST:

* Create a journal with pictures of your favorite moments that you can look through whenever you want to cherish your memories.

* Make something special out of something they owned. One of my favorite gifts I have ever received was a teddy bear my mom had made for me out of my granny's poncho and my favorite shirt of my grandfather's. It's so sweet because I get to hug it and get a little comfort whenever I need it. (You can go to www.memorybears.com to have a bear like this made.)

* Buy a star and name it after him or her. (Go to www.standup2cancer.org for more information.)

* Wear a piece of their jewelry, or create your own. (Sherry's girlfriends made cute beaded bracelets for us that said WWSD-- meaning "What would Sherry do?"--as a symbolic way to tap into her brilliant advice whenever we felt we needed it.)

* Do something that supports a cause that was meaningful to him or her. A girlfriend of mine trained hard and ran a marathon for lymphoma because her mom died from that disease.

* Write their biography so you can share their story with your own children years from now.

Honor Their Memory

I've been so moved by how many of you have found comfort by honoring the memory of the people you've lost. Each person in our lives leaves an imprint and changes forever who we are, and there's something so healing about celebrating that. It's such a beautiful legacy for you to create.

Here's what sixteen-year-old Michaela and fifteen-year-old Ashley wanted to share with you about how they honored the memory of friends they lost.

MICHAELA'S STORY: "We Get Together Every Year to Remember"

My friend Eric and I had known each other since we were seven years old. We were best, best friends; he was the person I went to with everything. You'd hardly ever see us apart... until the night he was killed by a drunk driver.

After the funeral, all our friends went to his grave every day for two weeks. Then his dad said he wanted to start having everyone come to his house every Monday night so we could talk about all the good memories of Eric. One time we all wrote letters to him and gave them to his dad to put into a book, which his dad read out loud on his birthday. Every year, on the date he died, we all get together and grill out and celebrate the person we loved. The very few who don't come are the ones who still have problems dealing with it.

ASHLEY'S STORY:

"We Did Something We Knew She Would Have Loved"

My friend had just gotten back from camp. I saw her on her way to soccer practice and said I was so happy she was home and that we should make a plan to get together. That afternoon at soccer practice something happened with her heart and she died right there on the field. It was so awful. That whole week my friends and I were all together to support each other. We wanted to do something in her memory, so we made a scrapbook for her and wrote messages in it to be buried with her. We also wrote to the guy who starred in the TV show she was obsessed with and told him about her and how much she'd loved the show. He wrote back to us and said he was going to find some way to honor her on the show, and then we saw that on an episode where he had to choose a number for his jersey he chose #12, which was her number. Doing things like that really helped all of us, because we were honoring the things in life that she loved.

#12

HEALING TOOL #3

Embrace the Gifts They Left Behind

There's a quote from the author Carol Crandall that I love: "You don't heal from the loss of a loved one because time passes; you heal because of what you do with the time." That says it all to me, because I think the only way to make sense of someone's death is to take what they meant to you and pass it along by living it, giving it, sharing it.

Every person we lose leaves behind gifts and lessons that make our lives richer for having known them. It's impossible to reduce my precious angels' magic in words, but just to give you an idea: from my granny I learned how to be a strong and independent woman; from my grandma Ceil it was the importance of bringing family together; from my mentor Roy it was about how to be fearless; from my loving mother-in-law, Susan, I learned how to have grace inside and out; from my friend Laura it was to be open to magic every day; and I've already told you about my dear Sherry.

The essence of each of these relationships was another part of my inspiration for creating *Ask Elizabeth.* What greater way to honor them than to share the very gift that they each gave me? They each reinforced for me that I had value, that my dreams could become real, that I was loved, that I was safe and that I had loving people to confide in. I know a lot of girls don't have that kind of support, and so I created something in the world so they would.

Being of service in this way allows me to pass along my loved ones' legacy and life force. On a day I'm missing them, I get to sit with you guys and use what I learned from them and pour it into my life . . . and now yours. You see how that flow of love can be kept alive?

You don't necessarily need to create something; it can just be about taking the lessons, wisdom, or inspiration you got from knowing them and carrying it forward in your life in a positive way. For seventeen-year-old Dylan, whose friend passed away after battling ovarian cancer, the gift was perspective. . . .

"My grandmother was my best friend, and when she died I lost the person I was closest to in the entire world. It's been ten months and I still can't get over it.... How do I?"

DYLAN'S STORY:

"She Completely Changed How I See the World"

When Amy died, I remember thinking, "Why would god do that? Why would he strip her of her childhood? She was so young." What was so amazing was that even though she knew she was probably going to die, her outlook on life was great. She was so sick with this for five years, and she was still going to school and playing sports and dealing with boys, and not letting it get in the way of that.

And for me, I'll have a Spanish test and think my week is hell... It really makes you think. It's kind of a blessing — I mean, not that her death is a blessing, but I feel like I live in reality now, not really worrying so much about little things, especially things I have no control over. What happened changed so many minds about petty stuff that was going on... I feel like she's this little angel who changed everything.

For sixteen-year old Jordana, who lost both her father and her brother, the lesson was to cherish and love the people in your life while they are here with you.

JORDANA'S STORY: I LIVE LIFE DIFFERENTLY NOW

When my father passed, we didn't have the best relationship. We butted heads on everything, and I can't remember if the last words I said to him were nice or defiant. He was a healthy, fit young man, so I figured we had all the time in the world to play this little love/hate game and make up when I grew up. His death was a shock, and it changed my life forever.

What my father's passing did was make me get closer to my brother. If I got mad at him, within moments I would let it go. I hugged him and told him I loved him more than ever before. I made it a priority to spend time with him; we created memories. So my heart isn't as heavy as it was with my father when my brother died, because while he lived, we loved! With my dad there is a load of unfinished business—enough unsaid words to fill a stadium. But with my brother, I said it all, so I can make peace with his passing.

What advice can I give? Forgive yourself for not being who you wanted to be when that person was alive, because you were doing the best you could and didn't know the time was so short. And then love the people who are still alive as much as you can. You might have lost someone, but as long as you are here, you have a second chance to make amends with those failing relationships that are in your life now. Say what you need to now!

Some of the last words my brother told me were: "Life is precious. Life is short. Live your life to the fullest. And I will always love you." I know that if I dwell on the pain and the grief, then I am not in the love. I am short changing what life can be, and that doesn't do his legacy justice. So I constantly remember that and take his inspiration with me wherever I go. The way I see it, I'm now living for two, so I gotta make it count.

It's so common to feel we didn't do enough while they were here.

"My grandmother was my best friend, and when she died I lost the person I was closest to in the entire world. It's been ten months and I still can't get over it.... How do I?"

FROM: me

TO: you

DEFINE THEIR LEGACY

If you need help figuring out the legacy they left behind for you, there are six things I created and wrote responses to that have helped me get clarity about each person I've lost. Here they are... Or create your own if you prefer.

* What I miss most about you...
* What I wish we could have done together...
* What I learned from loving you...
* One of my favorite memories with you is...
* The ways I am different now that you have passed....
* The ways I will live my life from here forward....

When you see what emerges from these, it will illuminate for you how you can begin to go forward in your life, knowing that their essence helped create who you are now and who you are yet to become. XOE

Remember

HEALING TOOL #4

Go Forward in Life as They Would Want You To

Seventeen-year-old Bailey's mom passed away when Bailey was fourteen years old. She said something so beautiful that I want to pass along to you: "After my mom died, my uncle told me that not only does my mother live within me, in my heart, but she also lives *through* me. So a big part of my healing was just trying to accomplish things that would make her proud, that she would have wanted to do, and get out her message to live life as if it's your last day."

How would the person you lost want you to live? What would they wish for your time here? Those are the key questions we can ask ourselves when we look toward building a new future.

Maybe you feel a little guilty for moving forward, but we always have to remember that new beginnings don't mean you forget about the person. You just take them along for the ride and know that they would want you to fulfill all your dreams and potential, and to be happy. Yes, you will carry the sadness of this loss within you and miss them, and still move forward in your life. As fifteen-year-old Alicia put it, "You'll always have that spot in your heart that knows this happened. That's okay, though, because it's a bittersweet reminder of everything that person was to you."

I'm sending you all my love for your healing.

Remember,
Carpe diem . . .
XOXOE

"My grandmother was my best friend, and when she died I lost the person I was closest to in the entire world. It's been ten months and I still can't get over it.... How do I?"

who am I?
who am I
secret worries
private thoughts and
secret worries
dreams
am I depressed
STAR
dreams
who I really am I?
4 SURPRISE
3 TRUST
2 JOY
1 HAPPINESS
DEPRESSION
6 SADNESS
8 ANGER
MY INNER WORLD
MOODS
VIEW-MASTER
am I happy?
secret worries
private thoughts
who I really am?
dreams and
my goals come true

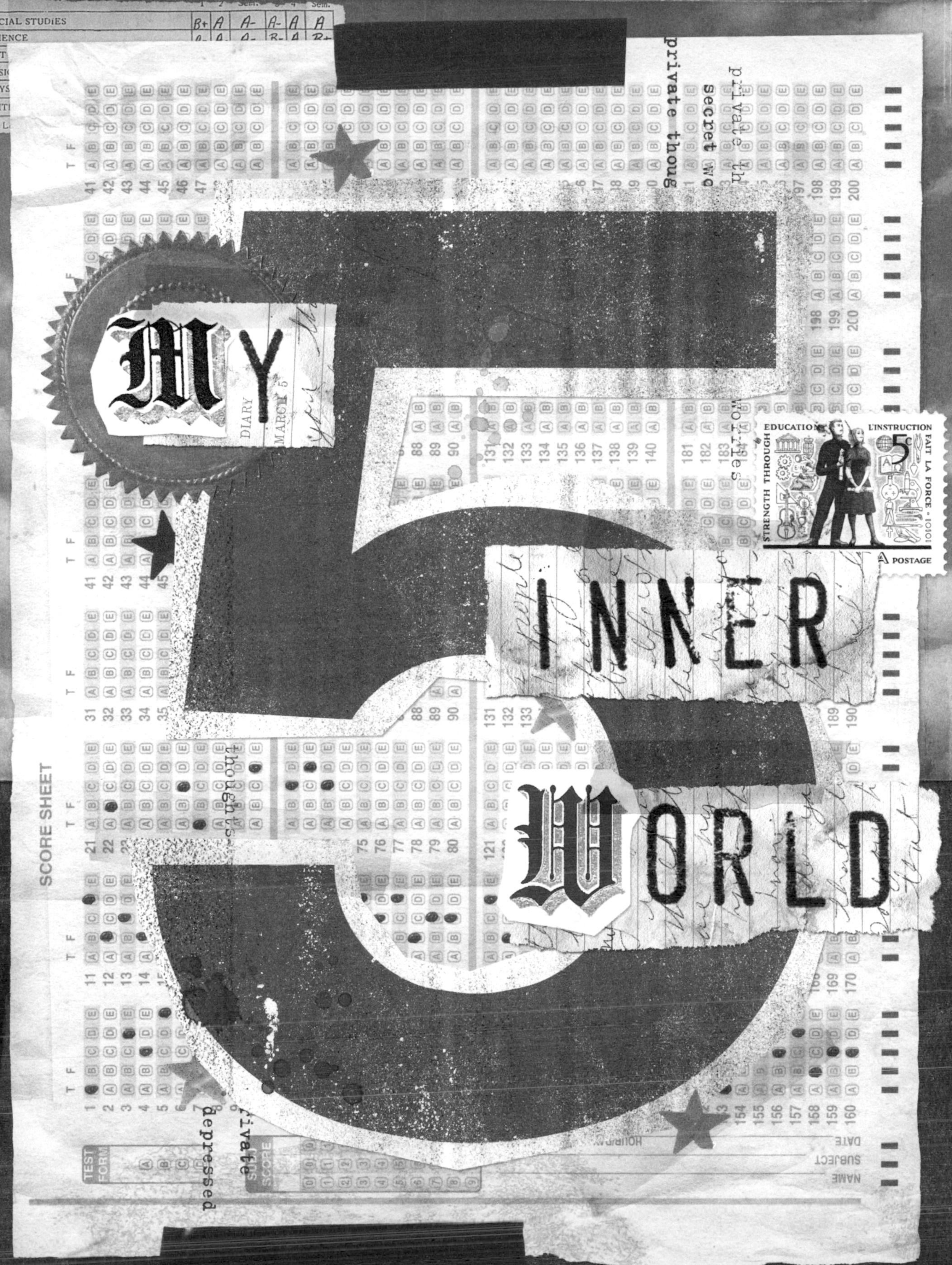

MY
INNER
WORLD
EDUCATION
L'INSTRUCTION
STRENGTH THROUGH
FAIT LA FORCE
5c
POSTAGE
private thoug
secret wo
DIARY
MARCH 5
SCORE SHEET
thoughts
private
depressed

PRIVATE THOUGHTS AND SECRET WORRIES

* *

At the end of the day, when we close our bedroom doors and tune out all the drama of our everyday lives, it's just us...and that's when those "private thoughts and secret worries" can creep in...

* Why do I feel so sad sometimes?

* Who am I?

* What do I stand for?

* What's my purpose?

* Where am I going in life?

* Will those dreams I have burning deep inside ever become real?

And so here, in our last chapter, I want to speak to those questions that lurk deep in our hearts, because ultimately, as you've known all along, this book is about you, and your inner soul is one of the most important parts of you. It's where your hopes, dreams, goals, and identity lie, all waiting to be discovered so that you can show up in the world as the amazing girl that you are.

So let's open up a deeper dialogue and look at what's really going on inside a lot of your minds....

How do I know if I'm in a bad mood or if I'm depressed?

No one goes unscathed

The annoying reality is that bad moods and mini-funks happen to all of us; that's just part of the ride. We all have days when we feel like no one gets us . . . when we just want to hide under the covers . . . when we're on edge and feel like we could snap at any minute. There's life stress, hormones, parent conflicts, relationship troubles—a whole mess of factors can bum us out on any given day. And then there's the underlying question: Will this bad mood ever go away?

PMS... don't get me started!

We're going to help you figure out ways to ease those normal, everyday bad moods, and how you can know when or if you're maybe heading into a darker place and need to get help. I promise, even though it might feel like you're all alone in the world on those bad days, you're not—your *Ask Elizabeth* sisters and I will always be right here on these pages, waiting to offer you our love and support.

Breaking Free of a Bad Mood

Even though it might feel that way, especially given the hormonal roller coaster we girls have to deal with, you are not a prisoner of your bad moods. Isn't that such a relief to know? As the smart *Ask Elizabeth* sister you are by now, you already know what to do to turn negative energy around, don't you? Flip it! (If you need a reminder about how to do this, see the question "What do you do when you look in the mirror and hate what you see?" in chapter one).

What usually helps me flip it when I feel stuck in a funk is activating a flow of grateful thoughts, kind of like we talked about in chapter one, only this time I'm focusing on my life as a whole. Like I'm grateful for my husband . . . for my family . . . my health . . . As soon as I start the thinking going in that direction, I start to feel better. Trust me, no mater how dark you're feeling, you can find at least a few things you're grateful for right now. This puts you back in the flow of life instead of fighting against it.

And then there's my best surefire flip of all time: exercise. When I'm in a bad mood, sad, or anxious, I need to do something physical . . . yoga, dance, cardio, whatever. Think about a bad mood as kind of like a clog in a pipe. Don't you have to get things moving to clear it out? Gross analogy, I know, but it's true; a bad mood is just negative energy that gets trapped, and we need to shake it up to get everything flowing again.

Exercise is like Drano for the soul!

Remember I mentioned my fantastic trainer Valerie Waters in chapter one? She has a brilliant saying that I've come to live by. She always says, "You're just a workout away from feeling better." So even if it's a day when I feel like I'm dragging myself to the treadmill or to Pilates, within ten minutes of exercise, I swear, I start to feel better. This doesn't mean that whatever it was that was causing the bad mood will magically disappear, but this helps change my mind-set so I can now approach the situation in a lighter, clearer way. Make sense?

Another flip for me is meditation. I won't lie, I don't always make time for this, but I can tell you that the days I take even five minutes to sit quietly and turn my focus inward, I feel much more grounded and peaceful. Then I'm able to be much more present with people I'm interacting with and more focused wherever I am, instead of having my mind race with anything else that's stressing me out. In the same way we recharge our cell phones with electricity, we all need to recharge our souls, and meditation is one of the best ways I know to tap into your power source and feel brand-new. Here's a collection of tips from girls on how they get back to feeling like themselves when a bad mood strikes.

THIS SPACE FOR WRITING

FROM: me

TO: you

CARD

THE ADDRESS

PLACE STAMP HERE

IT'S OKAY TO BE ALONE

So many of us feel afraid to just be alone with our thoughts and feelings; it's like a panic sets in if we don't have someone there that second to vent to. Of course having support from people who care about you is great, but being alone can give you an opportunity to process your stuff without the distraction of other people's opinions. It's also satisfying to know you came to an inner conclusion yourself!

Some of my friends tell me, "I can't believe you feel okay to sit and have tea by yourself—I feel so uncomfortable doing that." Honestly, those are some of the best moments for me to be able to reflect on what's going on in my life, head, or heart. Don't think you're a loser if you want or need a little time to yourself. Remember, you're your own BFF anyway, and you need "me time!"

XO E

GIRLS TO THE RESCUE

How we FLIP A BAD MOOD

I just sleep it off. I just get into bed, and in the morning, things always seem better.

Laura, 16

A LONG, HOT SHOWER AND A REALLY GOOD CRY ALWAYS DOES IT FOR ME.

-TINA, 18

Subject:

If it's something really petty that's ruining my day, I try to give myself a reality check. I ask myself if the situation is really as bad as I'm making it out to be. Stepping back from the mood and looking at it objectively takes away its power over me. —Maura, 17

Every time I get On my Horse And go riding, I get out of a bad mood and back into my joy. - Jillian, 16

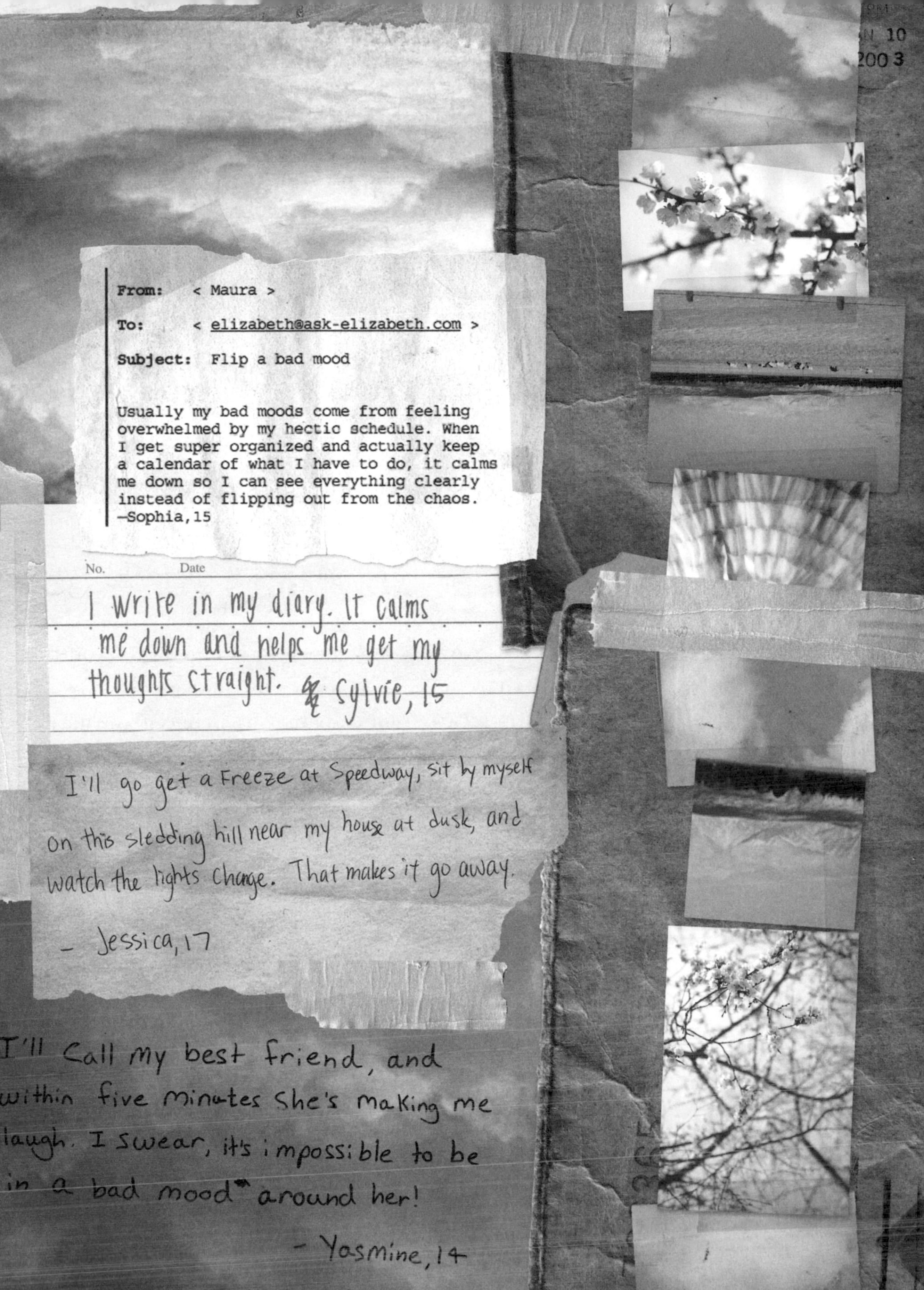

From: < Maura >
To: < elizabeth@ask-elizabeth.com >
Subject: Flip a bad mood
Usually my bad moods come from feeling overwhelmed by my hectic schedule. When I get super organized and actually keep a calendar of what I have to do, it calms me down so I can see everything clearly instead of flipping out from the chaos.
—Sophia, 15
No. Date
I write in my diary. It calms me down and helps me get my thoughts straight. ☆ Sylvie, 15
I'll go get a Freeze at Speedway, sit by myself on this sledding hill near my house at dusk, and watch the lights change. That makes it go away.
– Jessica, 17
I'll call my best friend, and within five minutes she's making me laugh. I swear, it's impossible to be in a bad mood around her!
– Yasmine, 14

When a Bad Mood Turns Dark

There are bad moods . . . and then there's actual depression, which is something that definitely needs more attention than just a mental flip. So how do we know when we're heading into a danger zone and need to get help?

For this question, Alissa Gunsberg—a wonderful psychotherapist who helps tons of teenage girls with tough issues—laid it all out for us. . .

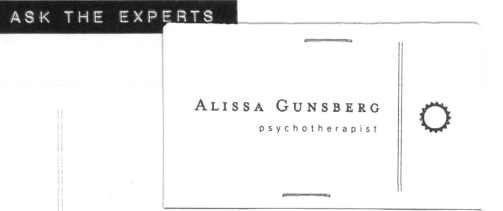

ASK THE EXPERTS

ALISSA GUNSBERG
psychotherapist

on

Bad Moods vs. Depression

Before we get in a bad mood about our bad mood, please allow me to make one thing clear. I have yet to meet a teenager who has never had an "I despise my life—I'm a loser—no one loves me—everybody hates me and I kind of hate them, too" sort of day.

We all have a beautiful "life flame" deep inside of us; sometimes it's just a little more fired up than others. You can expect the flame to be a little low every now and then, but what you really want to pay attention to is how long you've been experiencing negative feelings, and the intensity of your moods and emotions. If you're having serious trouble reigniting your flame for two weeks or longer, it might be a sign that you're feeling depressed and should seek out help (with the exception of the serious danger signs of suicide, which Elizabeth is about to list here—those signal that you need help immediately).

I know Elizabeth has resources listed on her website where you can turn for help—please use them. Depression, whether mild or severe, is an illness, and what you're going through can actually be treated. It's important to realize that although you're having a tough time, you're not the depression. It's separate from you, and you are not stuck feeling this way forever.

Let someone in your life that you love and trust know that you're struggling, so they can find a professional for you to talk to. A good therapist has so many ways to help depression! They can give you tools to help you reconnect to the joy in your life, or maybe even prescribe medication if you decide together that it's needed. We need to treat this illness so we can get that bright light of yours glowing again.

Alissa Gunsberg psychotherapist

I also consulted with two other well-known experts in the field of adolescent medicine, Elaine Leader, Ph.D., from Cedars-Sinai in Los Angeles and executive director of TEEN LINE, and Nora Helfgott, LCSW, a social worker from Mount Sinai Adolescent Health Center in New York City, who, along with Alissa, shared with me their information about the warning signs of depression. Depression is a serious issue, and I wanted to make sure you guys know what to watch out for.

☞ *You're struggling to focus in class, and feel extra tired and less motivated than usual.

☞ *You have much less patience; basically, you just don't want to deal with anything or anybody.

☞ *You have a harder time finding the energy and desire to be with people you love, and less enthusiasm to do the things that make you happy.

☞ *You feel a strong sense of loneliness, as though no one in the world understands you or what you're going through.

☞ *You feel like you just can't stop crying.

☞ *You feel disconnected from your true self and from the rest of the world.

☞ *Your sleep patterns might change; you might feel like you want to sleep all day or even not be able to sleep as soundly as you normally do.

☞ *You have feelings of being unloved and unworthy.

ANY OF THE FOLLOWING ARE SERIOUS DANGER SIGNS THAT SIGNAL YOU NEED HELP IMMEDIATELY.

☛ *You've given away important personal possessions or are writing out a will.

☛ *You don't want to plan for the future.

☛ *You feel hopeless (like thoughts that nothing really matters).

☛ *You have exhibited dramatic changes in behavior.

☛ *You have a preoccupation with death.

☛ *You have in any way thought of suicide (especially if you've created any kind of plan of how and when).

THERE IS NO SHAME
IN GOING TO THERAPY

I used to think that if I went to therapy, it would mean I was messed up. Like if I admitted I needed help, then that meant I failed or was weak. But as you already know, real strength is in giving yourself the support you need when you are going through something hard. With the right therapist or counselor, there is an opportunity for so much relief. You can express yourself so you don't keep everything bottled up inside, and you can get more tools to deal with what's happening. I promise you, talking to someone will make a huge difference in how you're feeling. Just trust me on this one, okay? You know I've got your back and wouldn't steer you wrong.

XOE

If you recognize yourself in any part of Alissa's description or this list of symptoms, please know you're far from the only one. Depression is more common than you think. I want to share a story with you from eighteen-year-old Caroline, who experienced depression firsthand and has some really wise thoughts about dealing with it.

CAROLINE'S STORY:

From: < Caroline >

To: < elizabeth@ask-elizabeth.com >

Subject: "I Realized This Wasn't Just a Bad Mood Anymore"

I went through a major depression my freshman year. I can't pinpoint any one specific event that led me into the downward spiral I was experiencing, but it got pretty scary. I started to completely shut down, even when I was with my closest friends. I felt like because nothing particularly traumatic happened, that there was no reason for me to be feeling the way I was feeling, and I beat myself up about it. I didn't have intense boy problems, my family was all alive and healthy, and I was doing okay in school. I was confused as to how I could be feeling so terrible. I cried a lot, and even got panic attacks sometimes. While some days I felt okay and like I could function, others I just couldn't. I thought maybe it was just a funk, so I kept it to myself. It took me hurting myself to realize that I had a real problem. I ended up turning to a teacher at school, who sent me to my counselor. He told my mom about the cuts on my legs, and she sent me to a psychiatrist. While talking about my problems was fine, I didn't feel better right away. I started to feel suicidal. I thought about it a lot- how I'd do it, when, if I'd leave my mom a note, how she'd react, etc.

It got the worst one day after school. Something that happened earlier must have put me on edge, but the entire day is so blurry in my memory. A fight with my best friend made me completely snap. I couldn't catch my breath I was crying so hard, and I ran downstairs, grabbed the first bottle of pills I saw from the medicine cabinet, and shoved almost two handfuls in my mouth. The aftermath is also fuzzy, but somehow my mom found out about what I had done, rushed home, and called poison control. Luckily, what I had taken wasn't lethal, but I spent the next two days doing nothing but drinking water to flush my system.

Immediately after, my psychiatrist put me on anti-depressants. I continued to beat myself up about my depression- I couldn't figure out why I had to put chemicals in my body to be normal. I thought I was weak. But when I started researching depression and mood disorders, I realized that some people are just born this way, and that it should be treated like any other disease. Eventually, my depression went away, but it took a lot of work. It wasn't just popping a pill every morning and saying things were okay. I pushed myself to start enjoying things, working out, and spending time with my friends. It wasn't easy and it wasn't quick, but it happened. The one thing to know about depression is that if you have it once, it's likely to happen again. It's good to be self-aware with your moods and be able to recognize when you are truly depressed, and to get help quickly. I can't imagine what my life would be like if I hadn't gotten help. To be honest, I may have tried to take my own life again, but I'm truly glad I didn't. While I do still struggle with my chemical imbalance, I have led a pretty great life, and look forward to continuing to do so in the future.

Whether it's a once-in-a-while bad mood or full-blown depression, the underlying message is the same: we're not at the mercy of negative feelings. There are so many ways we can lift ourselves up when our inner glow feels dimmed, either on our own or with help. You have way too much strength and smarts within you to let anything even dare try to extinguish that brilliant light within you. So please stay aware and in tune with your emotions, and do what you need to take care of yourself, okay?

Again, please, only the safe and healthy ways.

~~Will I ever~~

Will I ever
figure
out who I
really am?

Wow, what a question, right? I mean, it doesn't get much deeper than trying to tackle the biggest quest we're all here on this planet for: discovering who we are. You guys don't mess around!

You've asked so many questions about this, like:

* How do I figure out what matters to me?
* How can I be myself and not who people want me to be?
* Is it okay to explore a different side of myself?

All great questions, and all things that we'll discover, forget, and rediscover again and again on our journey. I can't even begin to tell you how many of you have talked about feeling pressure to figure it all out. As fifteen-year-old Carla said, "One week my hair is blond, then it's brown. . . . I'm into punk one week, rock the next. I just want to know who I am already. . . . I feel a little nuts, like I'm a different person every day."

But there's no rush here. Seriously! You truly don't have to nail the whole "Who am I?" question right now. Now's the time for you to try on as many changing identities and mind-sets as you want, and to try out different social scenes to see what feels right. It's the time for you to question if you're being yourself or who others want you to be, to create your belief system, and even to make some mistakes that allow you to find out what you will and won't stand for.

As sixteen-year-old Maggie said, "We're teenagers. . . we're supposed to be confused about who we are, because we just can't know yet. If you aren't confused, that's when I would worry!" So I say let's give ourselves a break here and have fun exploring all the different paths to discovering who we are. . . .

ACTION STEPS: Finding Ourselves

A lot of people think identity is just about how we look, what we wear, or even who we hang out with. But even though those are all great ways that we can express ourselves, and it's fun (and important!) to experiment to find what feels right, I think deep down we all know that none of those things are truly who we are. I love what seventeen-year-old Tia said about this: "There's this quote I love about how life isn't about finding yourself, it's about creating yourself. Whenever someone says they need to find themselves, I always say, 'What do you mean? You're right here! You've always been there on the inside. You just don't know how you want to portray yourself to the world, that's all.'"

Tia's right: the authentic you lives someplace deeper than whatever look we're rocking or scene we're into. She's in our hearts and souls, where we hold what we love, what we believe, what we're here in this world to do, and what we dream about. That, baby, is who you truly are! And we're going to give you some tools to help you find her.

ACTION STEP # 1

Identify What Matters to You

What's important to you? I know a lot of you have said that you have no idea, and I completely get how your desires and beliefs might all feel like a huge, confusing blur. But you actually have a lot more insight than you think into what matters to you! You might just need a little help digging underneath the surface to identify those things.

I have had the privilege of working with an amazing woman named Sharla Crow, who has also become a dear girlfriend. She created and owns a company called Seed, which helps people and companies realize their goals and dreams. She's helped me get clear on what matters to me and how to express that in what I create, which of course is a huge part of who I am. I wanted to share her wisdom with you, so that you can discover all the gifts, talents, and beliefs that make you who you are . . . and how you're going to express them in the world.

Here's the brilliant Sharla. . . .

ASK THE EXPERTS

SHARLA CROW

E-Mail: Sharla@TheSeedWork.com www.TheSeedWork.com

on Discovering Your Values

The process that I created to help individuals live their most authentic lives is called SEED™, because a seed is a simple yet powerful symbol. A seed holds within it the potential to become what it is meant to be. When we nurture and cultivate a seed, it takes root, grows and blossoms. Like a seed, you hold within you unique potential and purpose. Discovering your authentic self is about unearthing that potential.

So how do you begin? One of the most powerful ways is to define for yourself three core values that you will live by. A value is something that is of importance to you, a principle or quality of character that you find desirable and are committed to *being*. For example, you might feel particularly good when you are tutoring others. You see how you are able to contribute to another student's success, and this might lead you to discover that "sharing knowledge" is one of your core values. Perhaps your athletic pursuits have shown you how important it is to do your personal best, and you realize that "personal excellence" is another core value. Maybe you find particular joy when your friends are comfortable sharing their innermost thoughts with you, knowing you are "trustworthy."

Identifying core values lets you begin to cultivate your authentic self, and these values serve as your compass. When you have committed to personal excellence you are less likely to blow off studying for an important exam. When you are trust-

2934 N. Beverly Glen Circle No. 298 Los Angeles California 90077 • 310.472.9819 • www.TheSeedWork.com

worthy, you don't betray a friend's confidence. You begin to make choices based on who you want to be, not what is happening around you. Every time you connect to and act on your chosen values, you are cultivating your truest self.

Another way to discover who you are is to consider your gifts and talents. "Talent" is not just limited to things like having an exceptional singing voice, a remarkable athletic ability, or a gift for painting. Sometimes your unique gifts are so much a part of you that you don't recognize them. Beyond your obvious talents consider things you enjoy doing, things you are especially good at, and things that come easily to you. Don't limit your thinking! You might be particularly good at using social media to communicate. Maybe you excel at helping your friends pick out clothes with your innate sense of style or making people laugh—your gifts might be closer than you think.

Once you have a list of your unique talents and gifts, consider how you can use them to be of service. Take something that you enjoy and do well and use it to help others. Let's say you are great at using social media; perhaps you can set up a web page for your extended family and teach them how to use it so they can all keep in touch, or volunteer to set up a blog for the after-school tutoring program to inform students when a tutor is available. Acts of service like these allow you to live your values (sharing knowledge) and use your gifts (using social media and motivating others). One of the most amazing transformations I see consistently in my clients is how their lives flourish when they choose to use their gifts to be of service. Have you ever noticed how good it feels when you do something you enjoy *and* make a positive contribution? This is your authentic self at work.

So true... I can personally vouch to that

2934 N. Beverly Glen Circle No. 298 Los Angeles California 90077 • 310.472.9819 • www.TheSeedWork.com

ACTION STEP # 2

Open Up to New Experiences

I love nineteen-year-old Cassie's thought about discovering ourselves through experience. She said, "You're not just going to wake up one morning and know who you are. There are things that happen in your life, and you react to those situations, and that's how you start to know how you think, what you believe, and what you're capable of."

I couldn't agree more. When you try new experiences, a whole other side of yourself can show up that you never saw before, like, "Oh, hi, nice to meet you!"

Remember that Broadway play I told you about, where I had three days to learn the part? It was really intense, but it allowed me to discover that I'm someone who can deliver under pressure. A new part of my identity became "the girl who can handle whatever comes her way." Before then, people could tell me until they were blue in the face how much they believed that was true about me, but how would I have known for myself unless I walked through that experience?

Seventeen-year-old Dyanna shared a similar experience: "I know that if I need to examine my views on something, it helps to step outside the confines of my life. Like this past summer I went to a science program where no one knew me. Back home I was so used to people expecting me to be cynical, but I just went into the program feeling really positive and expressing that. It was so interesting, because I found out that I liked approaching life from a whole other perspective."

So go ahead and push yourself beyond your comfort zone. You might be amazed at the new side of yourself you find there.

ACTION STEP # 3

Let Go of Who You Are Not

Sometimes it helps to know who we *aren't* to show us who we are. I can tell you for sure who you are not:

* You are not your parents.
* You are not your brother or sister.
* You are not who people have told you that you need to or should be.
* You are not forever locked into being who you've been in the past.

It's pretty common for us to adopt specific roles or ways of being because it makes other people happy or fits their image of us. Maybe we're the funny one who makes people laugh, or the peacemaker in our family, or the smart one. But that's not helping us know who we are; it's only forcing us to fit the picture of what we think other people want us to be. And that can be a pretty lonely feeling, don't you agree?

Fifteen-year-old Lydia shared, "I don't think we can find who we are until we're willing to stop trying to be who everyone else wants us to be. I had this realization that high school is so short, and these people who are putting so much energy into meeting people's expectations are letting their youth go to waste. We all want to be accepted, but if you're not really being you, who is it that they're actually accepting?"

If the role you've been playing is getting old, or if you feel stuck having to live up to other people's views of you every second, it's time to let go of that so you can be free to express yourself in all your dimensions.

Here's seventeen-year-old Shane's story about that.

SHANE'S STORY:

"They saw me only one way"

I used to feel like people had this one-dimensional view of me, because I was the DO-GOODER GIRL (!!!). I was part of a volunteer organization, and that kind of became who I was known as, and I felt like I had to keep living up to that. One day, this one girl on the yearbook staff told me that they were talking about superlatives, and she said, "Well you should get NICEST." I was kind of offended because I CAN BE MORE THAN THAT! It made me think about my interactions with people . . . about how I was putting so much energy into being *nice* even though that's not ALL I was. After that, I tried to be a little more outspoken so I could break out of the image of this FRAGILE LITTLE NICE GIRL. It feels weird and good all at the same time.

Btw, sometimes when we are trying on something new, we tend to over-compensate until we find a good balance—just know that's okay!

Instead of being the person who others want you to be, now's your chance to make a shift in how you want to express yourself or approach life and become the person that you want to be.

ACTION STEP # 4

Learn from Your Mistakes

Mistakes aren't fun, and they're usually not pretty, but sometimes we actually have to lose our way in order to find ourselves. I know that might sound weird, but I'll explain so you can see what I mean.

You already know my story about being part of a movie early in my career that let's just say I'd hoped would turn out much better. When I landed that first movie role, I was so focused on the opportunity that I didn't let myself see how things started to go wrong or how I was being taken advantage of. Even though I knew deep down I wasn't being treated respectfully, I wanted to be professional and deliver whatever I was asked to do. I didn't know I had the right to speak up or how to take care of myself in moments when I wasn't comfortable. I abandoned myself over and over in the name of what I thought was my dream.

Understatement of the century!

Which somehow I equated with not making waves—yikes!

Through this experience or "mistake," I discovered that I would never give myself away like that again. So you see, for me, ultimately this wasn't about a movie succeeding or failing; it was about getting so strong that I would and could never betray myself in the future. I discovered that accommodating others at the expense of myself is no longer a part of who I am. Great! Lesson learned, right? And just when it seems you've got the lesson down, the universe will throw it back at you in a different way to make sure you got it. Don't worry, that's a good thing.... It's just to make sure you're solid.
--XOE

Even in everyday small ways! :)

I shared my story with you because it was one of the biggest detours from myself I have ever taken in my life, and I want you to know that those detours on the path are all part of the journey of getting to know yourself. We're supposed to make mistakes and become wiser with every step. As long as you make new mistakes and don't repeat the past ones, then you know you're heading in the right direction.

So don't be afraid—try on life! Allow yourself to have different experiences, viewpoints and ways of expressing yourself. Put yourself in new (but safe) situations that feel right to you and see what parts of yourself emerge. The exploration is the fun part. Will you make mistakes? Absolutely. But now you know that's okay.

ACTION STEP #5

Never Stop Evolving

Guess what? Even once you do figure out an aspect of who you are, it's going to change yet again. Remember, we're always growing. There's no arrival point on this journey, and if we keep looking for that, we're going to miss some really great experiences along the way. As sixteen-year-old Catie said, "I have to remind myself to 'enjoy being' sometimes . . . otherwise, I feel like more time will go by and I'll wonder where it all went."

So I say let's stop worrying about finding who we are and just let ourselves *be* who we are . . . moment to moment, day to day, year to year. And when some new experience or lesson or challenge comes along, you'll get to meet a whole other level of the real you. Trust me, she's pretty amazing!

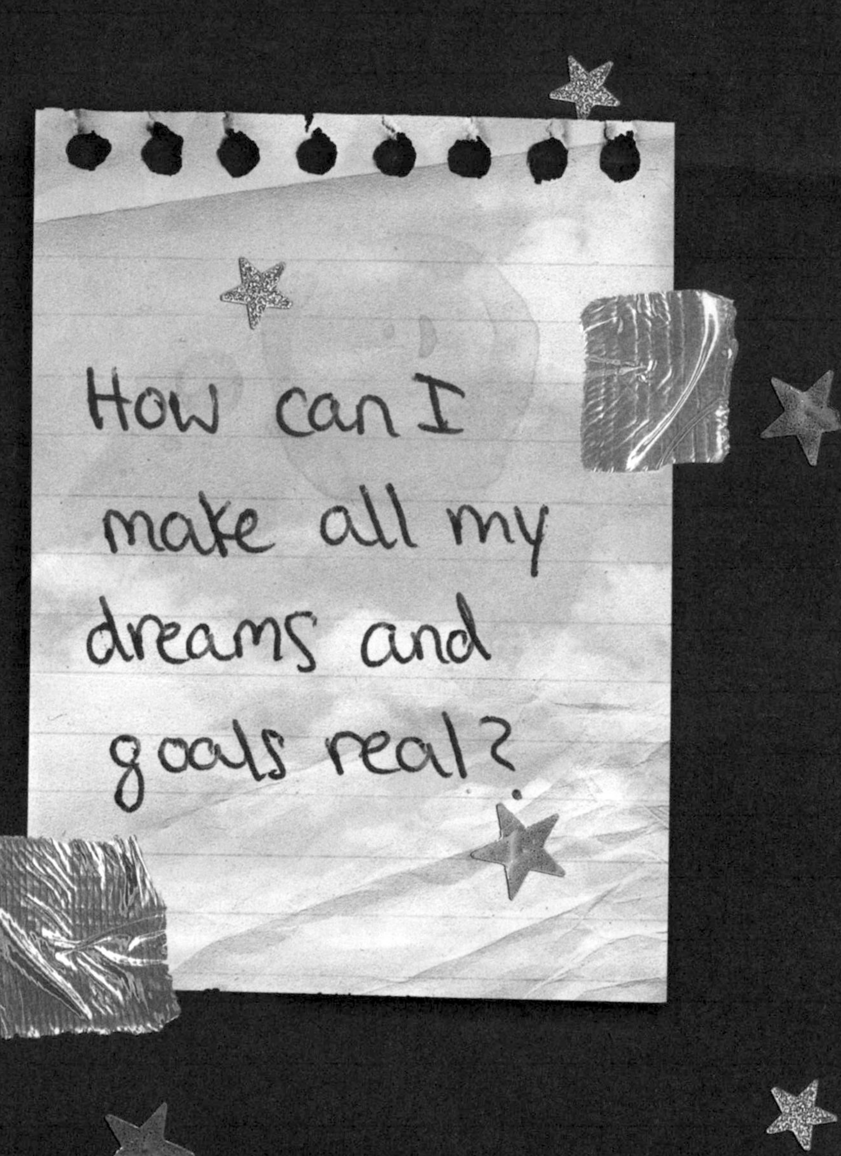
How can I
make all my
dreams and
goals real?

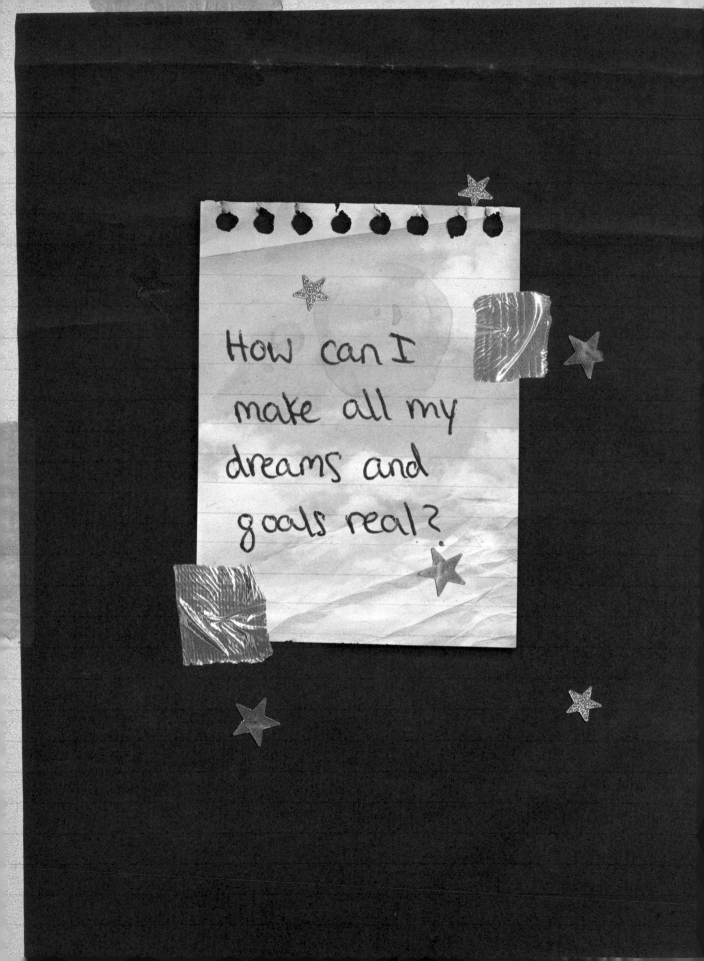

♡ It's ok if you don't fully believe it yet... you will once I get done with you! ☺

If there's one subject that is nearest and dearest to my heart, it's going after your dreams. I think you've probably figured out by now that I'm all about that! Whether you long to sing on the biggest stage in the world, go to college, or write a bestseller; I want you to let yourself dream big and believe that anything is possible. And as you carry that belief in your heart, ♡ your *Ask Elizabeth* sisters and I are going to share everything we know about fulfilling your highest goals and wishes, to help you on your way.

ACTION STEPS: Make it Real

It's not enough just to dream or to wish. . . . We need to actually put in the work to get where we want to go. A dream is only a wish if you don't back it up with action! So let's get right to it.

ACTION STEP # 1

Create and Hold the Vision

* What lights you up?
* What makes your heart sing?
* What makes you feel excited to get out of bed every day?

If you had an immediate answer to those questions, then you know that that's the thing you're meant to be doing. And if you didn't, don't worry. It's totally normal to not know yet. We all find our passions and dreams at different times. Just pay attention to that inner spark, whenever it shows up. . . and it will show up eventually! Every one of us has something divine within us that was put there to be expressed. When yours reveals itself, trust me, you'll know.

When the passion does show up, the key question is this: Where exactly do you want it to take you? What do your dreams look like in your mind's eye? There's so much power in being able to see exactly what you want, because then you can channel your energy toward that specific vision. Think about your goal as a literal destination: when you know exactly where you're headed, it's much easier to map out a route to get there, isn't it? I promise you, it really works. I know because I've lived it.

I've wanted to be a professional actress and dancer from...well, basically from the time I came out of the womb. My whole life, I've felt the happiest whenever I was acting, singing, or dancing. The joy I get from entertaining people, telling stories, and performing is what drove me, and still does.

The process of turning that dream into a reality began in the basement of my house in Michigan, long before I set foot on any movie set. There I had a tiny dance room with a dance bar, a pink lightbulb I put in as my "spotlight," and a poster on the wall of a ballerina that said, "If you can imagine it, you can achieve it." This was the space that held my dreams. I practiced alone every day in that little linoleum-floored room for hours, but in my mind I had a leading man and was surrounded by a chorus and a cheering audience. One day my imagination would take me to my Broadway opening, the next to the set of my own TV show or a movie premiere. Don't laugh--it was fabulous!

That doesn't mean I just twirled around in my basement and wished for things to happen. I worked my tail off! I took classes every day after school and practiced long, long hours for years, and took part in as many stage productions in my area as possible. The vision is where the dream took shape, and the work is what made it real. --XOE

If your dream is to perform, then create your own vision of yourself up on stage and see your name in marquee lights . . . and do the training and work to make that happen. If it's to get into a specific college, hang up photos of the campus someplace where you can see them every day, and picture yourself walking to class. And then, of course, do the research about what it takes to get into that school, and do it. If your big goal is to win a gymnastics championship, imagine yourself nailing your routine and holding up the trophy in front of the cheering crowd, while at the same time devoting your hard work and energy to train for it.

Get super-clear on your vision, and then just hold on to it for all you're worth. It's the launching pad for your beautiful dreams.

ACTION STEP # 2

Ignore the Naysayers

Sometimes our dreams can get extinguished by lots of judgments and fears that might not even be ours. If there's a voice in your head saying you can't or shouldn't go after something, I'd love for you to ask yourself whose voice it is. I mean, is it really you saying you can't or shouldn't go for it, or is it someone else's comments, fear, or judgment that you've adopted as your own?

A lot of people sabotage themselves, and don't even know it.

When you aim high and risk big, you might find that people try to hold you back—or even try to take you down. They might do it out of jealousy, or fear that you'll leave them in the dust, or maybe even because your courage to go after your dreams makes them feel small in comparison. Honestly, I don't care why they do it. I just don't want their negative comments to be the ones you get stuck on!

A lot of adults are unhappy because they stopped themselves at some point out of fear and let their dreams die, and no way are we going to let that

Here is what my goals are for the next 6 months:

1) Practice dancing a lot
2) Practice singing a lot
3) Do well in school

happen to you. Right here, right now, I say let's get rid of other people's negativity that you've taken on, and replace it with some new beliefs of our own.

People can throw at you what I call "dream crushers," which are those judgmental comments that can make you feel small or silly for even thinking you could reach for the stars. We can't control what people say, but you know whose reaction and beliefs we can control, right?

Something I like to do is create "dream rescue statements," which are inner mantras you can use as shields whenever those dream crushers come flying at you, threatening to extinguish your passion, vision, and belief. Here are a few examples, and of course you can create your own. . . .

DREAM CRUSHER:	DREAM RESCUE STATEMENT:
* "That's not realistic. It'll never happen." ☞	I am inspired by my dream, and I will stay committed to the focus and determination it takes to make it.
* "There are a thousand other girls just like you who are better at this." ☞	I have a gift, too, and I welcome the opportunity to better myself and become even more motivated by other girls who are striving the way that I am.
* "It's impossible to make that happen, coming from your background." ☞	I will do research and inform myself of the best instruction available to me, and I will create opportunities for myself to be around people I can learn from.
* "I just don't want you to be disappointed." ☞	I realize there will be ups and downs, and I welcome the chance to learn from all of it, wherever it will lead me.

See how it works? We have our own minds and hearts for thinking and dreaming. We can decide to not buy into their beliefs about what we "should" or "shouldn't" do or be and to create our reality as our own. It's up to us to take back control of the voice in our heads.

A lot of you have talked about how painful it is when the people who raise you don't give you their blessing to go for what you want. Or worse, actively try to stop you. That's why I want you to give yourself full permission to live the life you want, no matter what kind of background you came from or how many people tried to keep you down. You might need to move the mountains yourself, but when you do, you'll find like-minded people out there who support you on your path.

Sixteen-year-old Rosa shared, "My father constantly tells me I'm wasting my time with my art. One day he actually gathered up all my paintings and threw them in the garbage, saying, 'These are failure's dreams.' I had to find my own way to nurture my talent. Thank God for my art teacher at school, who let me use the art space there and stored my paintings for me."

I promise you, angels like this are out there... Never stop believing and searching for them!

Here's sixteen-year-old Chanel's inspiring story, for those of you who don't have someone in your life cheering you on.

From: CHANEL'S STORY:

To: < elizabeth@ask-elizabeth.com >

Subject: I Had to Be My Own Support System

It's not that my parents were cruel about my dream to be a singer, it's just that because they weren't able to achieve their dreams, they didn't think that I could. My mom had a record out in the seventies, and it didn't succeed. So whenever I said I wanted to be a singer, my mom would tell me I should be a teacher instead. If I sang in the shower, she'd tell me to "stop with that noise." It ended up stifling me for a really long time. . . . I'm just now starting to sing again.

Finding someone who believes in you is very rare. I came so close to giving it up, because people have a way of taking the light out of you. There was no one supporting me on auditions. My father even told me I sound like a man when I sing, or would tell me I'm not skinny enough to be onstage. The only thing that kept me going was reading inspiring stories about famous people who made it even though people tried to hold them back. It turned out that a lot of their early stories were just like mine.

I was recently watching a show on divas, and Mary J. Blige was talking about how when she was fighting all these demons, Aretha Franklin told her, "Get out of your own way." I guess that's what I would say to anyone who is afraid to take a risk of expression. . . . Just get out of your own way.

Another good tactic is to think of other people's doubt or disdain for your dreams as motivation; you can transform that negative energy into gold! I've decided to just let the naysayers in my life drive me even harder, to prove them wrong.

Here's seventeen-year-old Marissa's story about how that worked for her.

MARISSA'S STORY:

"Deep inside I knew they weren't right."

I used to follow what my friends said- like going out for cheerleading my freshman year instead of sports, which is what I really wanted to do. because they kind of convinced me I couldn't play sports. This past year, I felt like I really wanted to run for class president, but my friends said I couldn't do it because I was too shy. They literally said to my face, "You can't handle it."

I almost let it go, but I talked it over with myself and asked, "Are they right?" And from somewhere deep inside me I knew they weren't. That made me want to win a lot more. I wanted to show them- but more important show myself I could do this. I decided I wasn't going to let myself be someone who lets other people convince her she can't do things; I wanted to change that. And I did.

~~Oh,~~ And, oh, by the way... I won the election! :)

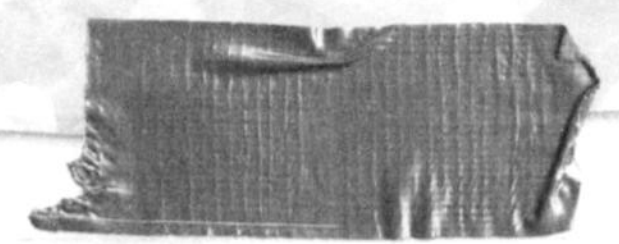

ACTION STEP # 3

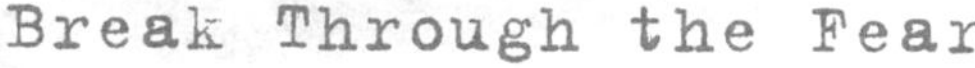

Break Through the Fear

Other people might try to keep you down, but that's nothing compared to what we can do to ourselves. As fifteen-year-old Samantha said, "Oh, I can't even begin to tell you how many golden opportunities I've said no to because of fear."

My dear friend Julian always reminds me to "get in the ring." There are definitely moments I have to talk myself into doing that! Sometimes I get nervous or question my ability or if what I want is even possible. But in those moments, I keep that quote in my head and make myself step up to challenges, because nothing ventured, nothing gained, right?

Courage doesn't mean that you're not scared; it means that you're afraid, but you're doing it anyway. For me, it comes down to allowing myself to feel the fear, stepping into what needs to be done, and having faith that all my prep work is embedded in me and will carry me through. I kind of have to hand it over to the universe in those moments and trust that it'll all be okay, no matter how things turn out. My acting coach and dear friend Howard Fine reminds me, "Have the experience—don't protect yourself from it." I usually remind myself that if I didn't care so much, I wouldn't be nervous. So in those moments, I hold on to being grateful that my passion runs that deep, and just leap.

Repeat that one more time—profound, right?

Want to hear how some of your sisters bust through their fears?

GIRLS TO THE RESCUE

How we

FACE OUR FEARS

2564 miles

I'm always afraid of failing, especially when it's something I'm passionate about. I'm scared I'm going to fall flat on my face and never be able to recover.

Whenever I feel that fear kick in, I try to remind myself that nothing is going to make the fear go away other than just doing the thing I'm the most scared of.

– Callie, 17

I always try to think of it like this: How do you know if you'd ever have succeeded if you don't try? You can't. You don't get another chance. So I say go back in time . . . take the chance and run with it. —Theresa, 17

No regrets, girls!

To: < elizabeth@ask-elizabeth.com >

Last year I started playing lacrosse. . . . It sounds like a little thing, but it was something I'd always wanted to do but was too scared to, because in my town, if you don't start at a young age, you can't keep up because everyone is so competitive. Two friends and I decided to try it together, and I think having them there by my side, doing it with me and encouraging me, really helped. —Jacklyn, 15

I come from a really successful family, and I'm afraid I won't be able to measure up, so, like, why even try? But lately I've decided that I don't have to do it the same way or on the same level. My success or failure is my own. When I realized that, I wasn't afraid to go for it. —Stella, 16

To: < elizabeth@ask-elizabeth.com >

For a long time I was afraid that it wouldn't be possible to go after my dreams because I come from nothing. Like I just figured, 'I guess that's just who I'll always be.' A teacher of mine believed in me and put me in a photojournalism project. It changed my life. I saw how I could be good at something I really loved, and that gave me the courage to keep going. Now I love this quote: 'Don't waste another day not doing what you dream of doing.' It doesn't matter what you come from. Be the first to go for it. . . . The way I see it, I'm also setting the example for my little sister and cousins. —Zonia, 14

ACTION STEP # 4

Overcome the Obstacles

Wouldn't it be so great if we just followed our passion and everything fell right into place?

As much as we would love that, the path to achieving whatever it is that we want usually isn't a straight line. There will be times that you get derailed or that you feel like you want to give up. I'm not saying this to be negative; I think you know by now that the last thing I would ever do is discourage you! I just want to arm you with ideas to help yourself in those challenging moments that inevitably happen. I like to think of those as tests from the universe to make sure we really want whatever it is that we're striving for.

Whenever I hit an obstacle, my dad has always said, "Let's just remove those roadblocks." Smart dad, huh? Here's twenty-year-old Darci's story of how she removed the roadblocks that might have stood in her way.

DARCI'S STORY:

"I Knew it was the Place for Me"

As soon as I first visited NYU, I knew it was the college I was supposed to go to. The day I found out I had been accepted was seriously one of the highlights of my life thus far.

There was only one thing that I was worried about, and that was the money it was going to cost me. ~~Between~~, the financial aid package and the money my mom had saved, it looked like I would only have enough to last me for two semesters. For my first year, I spent a lot of time stressing over money, but no way was I giving up on this dream. During my winter and spring breaks, I went back to the restaurant where I worked and waited tables. Over the summer, I worked 40 hours a week, which didn't leave a lot of time for friends, but it was worth it.

My second year I actually had to take a semester off because I couldn't afford it and it was one of those events I hyped up in my head as being completely cataclysmic; I thought my world was going to end. Surprise—it didn't. I'm now a full-time student again and taking the financial struggle one step at a time. My strategy now is just making sure I have enough to cover the next semester, and not getting too ahead of myself. I know I will graduate from NYU one day—it will just take me a little bit longer than others. Taking a chance and going here was super-scary. On the other hand, thinking about passing up the opportunity to go to NYU was pretty scary as well!

What's standing in your way? Whatever it is, I know you're smart enough to figure your way around it. Do whatever you need to do: research, ask for help, try an alternate route. Just keep going with all your passion, and that obstacle won't stand a chance.

ACTION STEP # 5

Be Flexible

Sometimes a dream doesn't turn out exactly as we imagined. I know it can seem like an obstacle, like, "Hey, this isn't what I originally pictured, so what's happening must not be right." This will just take some flexibility; the picture that emerges might look different, but it can be just as good—or better—than you originally imagined. Don't block the flow of where you're meant to go! ♡

Here's fifteen-year-old Michelle's story about shifting her vision so that it still fit her underlying desires.

MICHELLLE'S STORY:

"That I Got to Dance is what Mattered... Not the Method"

I've been dancing since I was 3 years old and was extremely committed to ballet. I LIVED and *breathed* it, and it was all I ever wanted. My friends would say I eat, sleep, and do ballet. When I was twelve or thirteen, though, I really **struggled** with body image issues, which derailed my dancing and made me feel like I couldn't dance just because I wasn't PAPER-THIN like the other girls. I really wanted to become involved in a core company but didn't feel CONFIDENT or comfortable dancing among other ballerinas. I overcame these issues by researching other styles and exploring other types of dance, like MODERN and LYRICAL where strength and technique are critical rather than *size*. I'm now a member of a modern dance youth company that performs **ALL OVER** the East Coast. I actually love it now even MORE than ballet. ♡

As you're going after what you initially set out to do, you might decide to change your original vision into something else, and that's okay. Maybe it's your heart that calls you to try something different or new. The changing vision isn't a failure; as long as it's something that gives you joy, it's just a new door opening. Dreams can shift, and a better opportunity can sometimes be staring you right in the face.

One of my mentors, Sherry Lansing, came from Chicago to Hollywood to make it as an actress. Little did she know her path would ultimately lead her to becoming the head of Paramount Pictures—ironically, a position in which she held more power than any performer. Instead of using her creativity as an actress, she used her creative talents and leadership to make a huge impact on the movie industry from a whole other direction.

Often the skills you nurtured still serve you, so nothing you did was ever a waste.

Inspiring, right?

ACTION STEP # 6

Keep Yourself Motivated

One of the biggest challenges we can face is our own ability to stay focused. Let's be honest: it's hard to do that when we all have such busy schedules and there are so many distractions, or when we feel discouraged, or even when things don't happen as quickly as we want them to. Believe me, I get it, . . . I know you want it, and you want it yesterday!

It's so hard sometimes to trust the timing, and the process of getting where you want to go. But look back on anything in your life that worked out: even though it might have been frustrating in the moment, didn't everything ultimately happen just as it needed to? One twist or turn of events and the outcome wouldn't be what it is now, which is what fifteen-year-old Sara saw:

I like to call that "divine time."

"I play the violin, and I tried out for the community orchestra my freshman year. I was so disappointed when I didn't make it, but it just made me work even harder that whole year, and I got soooo much better. So when I tried out as a sophomore, not only did I make the orchestra, I got solos. The girl who was always chosen to perform solos had gone off to college, and now because of my hard work I was good enough to be chosen for them. Yeah, I hated having to wait, but looking back, I wasn't really ready yet. It was so much more rewarding to know I earned my place. It was more satisfying to come back and be one of the best."

No one is ever going to hand you your dreams. Honestly, it is so much sweeter to experience them when you know what you put in to get there. It's so hard, I know, but I have definitely learned that any dream worth going after takes work, patience . . . and faith! Trust that if you are doing everything necessary, everything is unfolding as it should.

What helps me stay on track is having clear intentions. For instance, for *Ask Elizabeth,* my intention is to be of service and (as you know) empower girls. That focus helps give me direction and keeps me right on track with my vision. When I see your lives being changed through our exchange of love, wisdom and support, that fills my heart with the most unbelievable sense of joy. And what could possibly be more motivating than that?

In moments when you need a boost of motivation, try to connect back to what it is that you love about your passion and the deeper reason you're pursuing it in the first place. Is it the joy it brings to others? The deep sense of personal pride and accomplishment you get from living up to your full potential? Making a difference in the world? (If you need some guidance on finding your purpose, take a look at Sharla's great advice in the question "Will I ever figure out who I really am?") Think of your mission like a strong magnetic current that runs through you; when you tap into that current, you'll attract the people, ideas, and energy you need to keep moving forward.

Here's how other *Ask Elizabeth* girls keep themselves motivated.

GIRLS TO THE RESCUE

How we STAY ON TRACK

From: < Miranda >

To: < elizabeth@ask-elizabeth.com >

One of the biggest things that gets in the way of me (or anyone, I think) reaching my goals is when I start not believing in myself. So every day I try to do something good for someone else, and for myself. That helps me to think I have a purpose, and once that confidence kicks in, talent flows much easier. —Miranda, 18

For me, I think about the alternative. Like if I don't stay focused and determined with my grades, where does that leave me? I'm not saying my life would be horrible if I didn't go to college, but I know that having that education will give me more choices, and I want that.
—Rachel, 16

From: < Zoe >

To: < eli[illegible]eth.com >

My older sister is a model person and student, and so whenever I think of giving up I talk to her and try to follow her lead. Having a role model like that in my life helps so much.... I think it's good to try to find someone who you want to be like, and take inspiration from them. —Zoe, 16

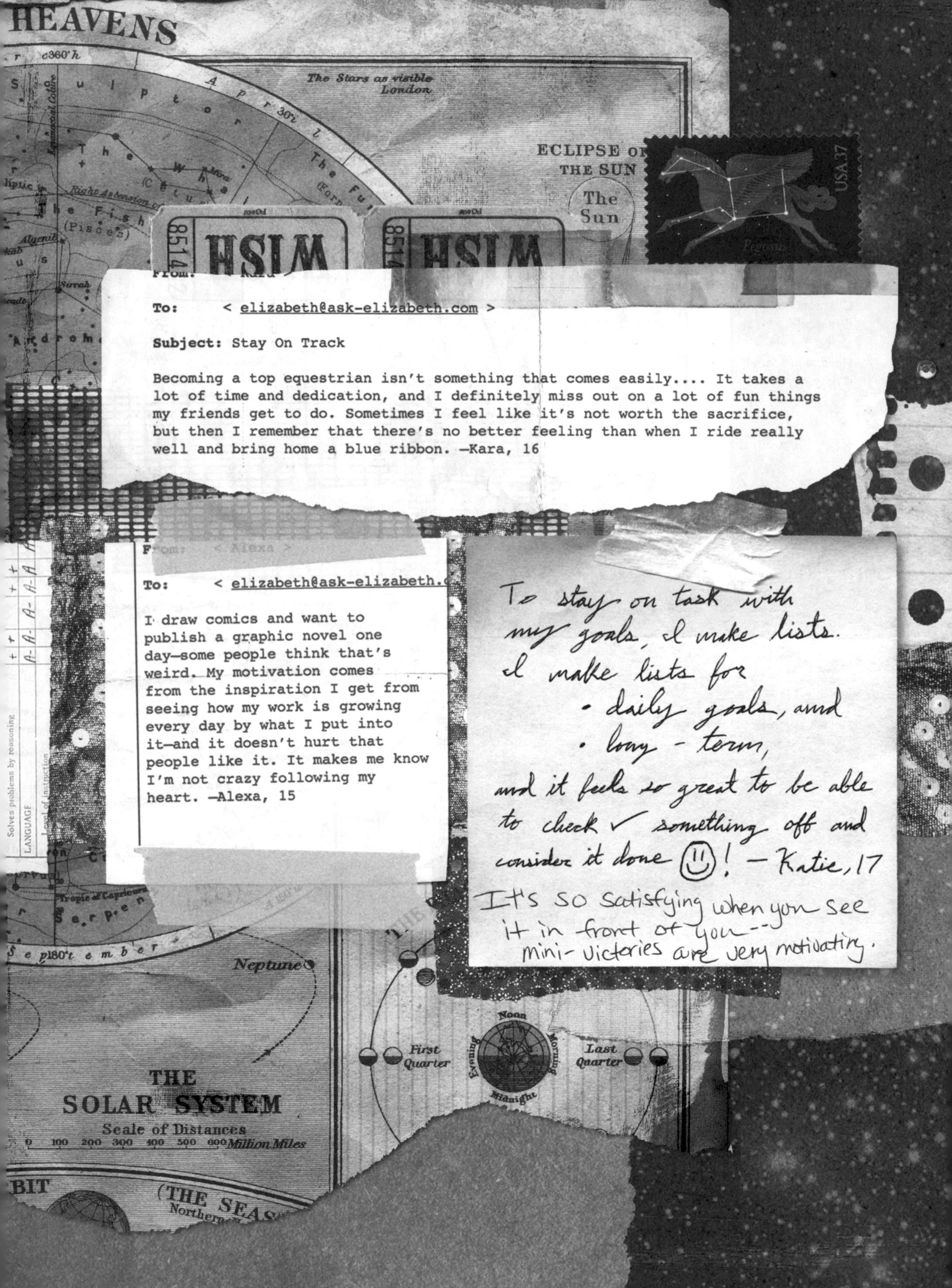
To: < elizabeth@ask-elizabeth.com >

Subject: Stay On Track

Becoming a top equestrian isn't something that comes easily.... It takes a lot of time and dedication, and I definitely miss out on a lot of fun things my friends get to do. Sometimes I feel like it's not worth the sacrifice, but then I remember that there's no better feeling than when I ride really well and bring home a blue ribbon. —Kara, 16

From: < Alexa >

To: < elizabeth@ask-elizabeth.c

I draw comics and want to publish a graphic novel one day—some people think that's weird. My motivation comes from the inspiration I get from seeing how my work is growing every day by what I put into it—and it doesn't hurt that people like it. It makes me know I'm not crazy following my heart. —Alexa, 15

To stay on task with my goals, I make lists. I make lists for

- daily goals, and
- long-term,

and it feels so great to be able to check ✓ something off and consider it done ☺! —Katie, 17

It's so satisfying when you see it in front of you— mini-victories are very motivating.

I grew up really poor, and no one in my family has ever been a success. As hard as it's been, the thing that keeps me going for my dreams is how much I want to make a different life. I want to make it easier for me and my family one day. -Karina, 15

At the end of the day, finding out who you are and what you're here to contribute to the world is what life is all about. That's the process of discovery that gives our lives so much meaning. So please open your mind, heart, and soul to all the amazing opportunities out there for you to grow and experience life. I think sixteen-year-old Isis so beautifully lives this. She said, "I have a never-ending imagination and a heart full of dreams and desires. . . . That's who I am. That's why, when I'm older, I just want to experience everything, whether it's a profession, a country, a food, a house, a person, or even a climate that comes my way. I want to try it all! I just want to live my life to the fullest and experience everything I can, both the challenges and the fun stuff, because all of it makes me grow. I want to be happy and share that happiness with others. That's a meaningful life to me."

A Final Thought From me To you . . .

There's a beautiful quote from my friend and inspirational author Marianne Williamson from her bestselling book A Return to Love that says, "It is our light, not our darkness, that most frightens us. We ask ourselves, who am I to be brilliant, gorgeous, talented, and fabulous? Actually, who are you not to be?"

We can stumble in our darkness and cling to our fears, but truly, we're the only ones who are keeping ourselves from radiating our brilliance. Like I said in the opening pages of this book, you are here in this world to let your unique light shine. Why deprive yourself and the world of that?

It is my deepest wish that you take all the insights and ideas you learned here in these pages and go out there to share the amazing gift that is you. Let's pass along the beautiful energy, love, and support of the Ask Elizabeth sisterhood that you're now a special part of in as many ways as we possibly can.

You're going to light up this world.... I know you will! And I'll be sending you love and Ask Elizabeth power every step of the way....

Love, light and magic,

XOXO Elizabeth

THANK YOU FROM THE BOTTOM OF MY HEART... GREGGIE: to spend my life with you is the greatest gift of all. Thank you for knowing I needed to take the leap to create Ask Elizabeth and for waking me up to what my heart was longing to express and offer. You knew it before I did. Thank you for your tireless artistic vision and help on designing this baby and for you seeing me more clearly than I see myself. I love you-forever... • **MOM AND DAD:** for being the most amazing parents ever—how blessed I am to have been given YOU...for taking my dreams seriously and always letting me know everything is possible—I couldn't do it without you • **JASON:** For loving me and being the best big brother a sister could ask for • **MY ANGELS, RGPWSS:** I miss you everyday. I carry you in all I do and all I am becoming. Love, light and magic. Waaa power forever... • **JERRY LAUREN:** for your love and never-ending support • **DEBRA GOLDSTEIN:** for being the most amazing collaborator I could ever ask for. There is no one I would rather have gotten lost in the back woods of Kentucky with! Thank you for your love, talent, commitment, professionalism, tireless passion and for helping to fulfill my dream. I am forever grateful to you. • **EMMA:** for sharing your Mommy with me • **ALL THE GIRLS WHO CONTRIBUTED:** you know who you are...I love you. I couldn't have done this without you. Thank you for your time, energy and for being courageous enough to share your own life experience and wisdom in the name of being of service to other girls. Your voice matters and will change lives...I wish the editing process could allow every word, but then we'd have volumes. Know that whether your words are on these pages or not, you influenced this entire journey and the love you poured into this process, created a powerful message that affects all who read this. I am blessed to know you. • **MATTHEW ELBLONK:** for your support and for protecting me and guiding me every step of the way. You are more than an agent—you are a superhero. • **ADAM GRIFFIN:** for believing in my ideas and goals—however "outside the box" • **DARIN FRANK:** for going to the mat for me • **JULIAN SCHLOSSBERG:** for not forgetting me that day at the Promenade and for being there for me with the perfect words in the moments that count...and all moments with you do. • **HOWARD FINE:** for making me see my worth. I treasure our friendship, inspiring work and laughter in the rain • **MY GO TO GIRLS: JENNIFER BEALS, CARLA GUGINO, SEANE CORN, DANA KLEIN, KATIE MITCHELL, KATHY FRESTON, BROOKE WEISBARTH, AMY NICKIN, LAYLA DANLEY, ELE KEATS, PARKER POSEY, MERRYN JOSE, DYLAN LAUREN:** for your constant support throughout this process and as we walk this path together—and for showing me that there are amazing women that can have your back like nobody's business. • **SHARLA CROW:** for helping my seeds to blossom. • **GIRLS AT OWLAG:** you inspire and move me and I thought of you everyday as I wrote this • **OPRAH WINFREY:** for being an example that the light only shines brighter when you do everything with love. I will forever carry the honor of you letting me know your "daughters". • **SAUL CHOZA:** for our authentic, magical exchanges...and surrender • **JO GARTIN:** for your love, luck and angels and for your time, support and creativity. • **BEVERLY BERG PhD:** I am eternally grateful for your love, guidance and insight • **PHIL STUTZ:** for teaching me how to be a warrior when I needed it most, and for the tools that keep on giving • **ANNA STROUT:** for your friendship and for believing in Ask Elizabeth from day one • **ROY LONDON, MR. LASCU, MISS BARBARA, LAURA HART, DIANE HARDIN, NORA ECKSTEIN:** there are no words for how you helped shape my life and my art • **ALL THE EXPERTS:** for your generosity of spirit and for taking time out of your own busy schedules to share your wisdom and insight that grace these pages and my website. • **EVERYONE AT PENGUIN PUTNAM: STACEY BARNEY** for believing. To **DON WEISBERG** for supporting me in a way that any author would wish for and for allowing my dream to become a reality on these pages. To **DAVID BRIGGS** and **JENNIFER BESSER** for your tireless enthusiasm and devotion and for making sure this baby maintained the integrity and vision I hoped for. You are my heroes. • **PAUL KEPPLE & RALPH GERONI AT HEADCASE DESIGN:** I cannot begin to thank you enough for bringing these pages to life—for going above and beyond and making it your mission to deliver the picture in my head and heart. Thank you with everything I've got for your brilliance, artistry, vision and hard work you relentlessly poured into this book. • **A SPECIAL THANK YOU TO MY FAMILY AND ALL THE AMAZING SOULS WHO HAVE LOVED ME AND HELPED ME ALONG THE WAY AND TO THOSE WHO HAVE CONTRIBUTED TO ASK ELIZABETH: DR. ANGELA DIAZ, MT. SINAI ADOLESCENT HEALTH CENTER, BINDI, NANCY LUBLIN, SHERRY LANSING, LISA KUSSELL, CHRISTINA PAPADOPOULUS, FRIENDS AT LE PAIN QUOTIDIAN, SANRIO, DAVE MARCHI, EXHALE, SUGAR PAPER, KRISTAN SERAFINO, ALANA EMHARDT, SHANNON CONNOLLY, JAYCEY STAMLER, KATIE HAYEK, SARA LOWRY, JULIA KEHELLER, FONDA SNYDER, EDEN WEINBERG, KERRY LEA, LAUREN BUSH, SABRINA WARD HARRISON, DAVID LAUREN, OSCAR COHEN, JENNY LAUREN, AUDREY BERKLEY, ALLISON FREERS, MOLLY KALLINS, MELISSA ROCCO, ANNIE BLANKENSHIP, JENESIS SCOTT, FRANCES FABIAN, SABRINA FANI, STEVEN RUBENSTEIN, BRETT RAMEY, BLAINE HALVORSON, ERIC CAHAN, ENDRE NAGY, JON VASQUEZ, DAYLE BREAULT, EUGENIA WESTON, TARYN & KATE MAITLAND, DIVINE BRADLEY, CYNTHIA BAIN, GEOFFREY CANADA, MARIANNE WILLIAMSON, TRAVIS NEESE, LAUREN COHEN, CINDY MORI, JILL BARANCIK, ROBYN MILLER, MARLENE KELLY, YOGAWORKS, CAITLIN MCARTHY, LAURI HARRIS, IVAN HAGEMAN, EDGE PAC, KRISTIN FRAISSE, BARYSHNIKOV ARTS CENTER, EMILY ROBINSON, ALLIE BEACH, MORGAN & MYA JONES** and to all the amazing schools, organizations, teachers, guidance counselors, principals, moms and dads that let your extraordinary girls participate and allowed me the honor of working with them.

ELIZABETH BERKLEY is an accomplished actress who has appeared on television, in film and on Broadway. She recently recurred on CSI:MIAMI for two seasons and her numerous other credits include ANY GIVEN SUNDAY and THE FIRST WIVES CLUB. She is still recognized for her starring role in the teen hit comedy SAVED BY THE BELL, which thanks to television syndication has made her an admired favorite amongst a whole new generation of teen girls. Now Elizabeth is making connections with her big sister-style of communication with these girls through Ask Elizabeth, her not-for-profit organization that includes self-esteem workshops, and a thriving website (www.Ask-Elizabeth.com) that have translated into a nationwide movement. This journey has inspired ASK ELIZABETH, her first book for teen girls. She was a featured contributor on Oprah.com, bridging the communication gap between mothers and daughters.

Elizabeth is married to artist Greg Lauren. They divide their time between New York City and Los Angeles.

Why is it that even when people give you compliments, you still feel ugly?

HOW DO YOU KNOW IF A FRIEND IS FAKE?

What should you do if you feel like you're drifting apart from a friend?

How do I Learn to be myself around people?

"what can I

WHY ARE GIRLS SO JUDGMENTAL OF EACHOTHER?!

I HATE MY BODY!! HOW CAN I Love MYSELF?

How do you know you like someone?

What do you do about jealous girls?

How do you deal with a friend who is getting mad at you because she is in a bad mood?

I feel like my best friend is changing. What should I say to her?

How do you deal with the feeling that your friends or family do not appreciate your accomplishments?

backstabbing friend

self-conscious about my body. I don't want to about myself. I want to like my body. How??

Why don't I ever feel wanted or needed?

HOW DO YOU KNOW WHO TO REALLY TRUST?

...t do you do if someone is jealous of you and they are taking it a bit overboard?

Do you think you can ever change a person? LIKE... the way they are or live their life?

How do you boost your self-esteem when there is always someone better around?

I'm scared of the future—how can I deal with this?

How do you feel when you get a boyfriend?

What is it like to be in LOVE?

How would you deal with negative comments being said to you?

How do you choose what you want to do in life?